PRIEST IN THE PIAZZA

PRIEST IN THE PIAZZA

Touchline tribute to a Council

by

BERNARD BASSET, S.J.

With illustrations by
PENELOPE HARTER

THE CATHOLIC BOOK CLUB
121 CHARING CROSS ROAD
LONDON W.C.2

DE LICENTIA SUPERIORUM ORDINIS

NIHIL OBSTAT: JOANNES M. T. BARTON, L.S.S., S.T.D.

CENSOR DEPUTATUS

IMPRIMATUR: ✠ GEORGIUS L. CRAVEN

EPISCOPUS SEBASTOPOLIS

VIC. CAP.

WESTMONASTERII: DIE 4ᴀ APRILIS 1963

The Nihil obstat *and* Imprimatur *are a declaration that a book or pamphlet
is considered to be free from doctrinal or moral error. It is not implied that those
who have granted the* Nihil obstat *and* Imprimatur *agree with the contents,
opinions or statements expressed.*

*All the Royalties from this book are to be devoted to the
Nevett Fund for Indian Children. See Epilogue (p. 105).*

*The author acknowledges with thanks permission
from the Editor of the* Catholic Herald *to use those
portions of this book which originally appeared
there.*

MADE AND PRINTED IN GREAT BRITAIN BY
BILLING AND SONS LIMITED, GUILDFORD AND LONDON

CONTENTS

SETTING THE STAGE

IT has not been easy to resist the temptation to write all these articles afresh. One could polish them up, unsplit their infinitives and, in the quiet of a Bournemouth presbytery, add further details not observed in Rome. With the help of a dictionary of quotations I could have stepped up the culture and inserted several edifying thoughts.

For good or for ill, I have been advised to limit alterations to the spelling and arrangement of the book. Newspaper articles require adjustment before they appear in book form. Cross-headings have to be removed and I have used the chance to restore certain details which had to be omitted for want of space. I am assured that the very lack of last-minute polish will save the spontaneity of what I wrote. As on the kitchen front, for all the garnishing with herbs and sauces, tripe remains tripe.

Need I say that the chance of being in Rome at the time of the General Council will remain one of the greatest and happiest events in my life. I was only a 'hanger-on', part-time assistant at Vatican Radio and with a roving commission from the *Catholic Herald* to poke about and record what I liked. I chose to avoid the more profound and theological work of the Council, for Rome was filled with scholars who are, no doubt, at this very moment busily writing books. The very greatness of the Council may justify more trivial comment on the general Roman setting by an English priest, gripping his umbrella and crouching in the wings.

A commentator must make a conscious effort to be honest and to use those literary liberties of imagination to present an accurate picture of the scene. No one accuses an artist of dishonesty if he heightens certain colours to convey the true vivacity of the subject which he is striving to depict. Some of the essays here are factual, some seek to convey an impression, some are completely fictional but based on observed fact. I was not consciously imitating anybody and yet nearly every detail happened in one setting or another and you must judge if my picture of Rome is true to life.

There are, alas, sure to be some who will be shocked by the laughter, finding it, in the solemn and sacred setting of the Council, ill-judged and out of place. Yet those who know Rome will also know that laughter is always round the corner and that the very greatness of the Council created an air of happiness and humour not found in more trivial events. I never laughed so much or cried so much or prayed so much as in the two months of the Council session and it would be hypocritical to disguise the fact. My picture will be false only if it offends against the charity which was so marked a feature of the Council or fails to convey a deep, filial

2

love for the Pope, the bishops, all Christians a
Mother Church.

OCTOBER 11TH, 1962

I write this on the afternoon of Thursday,
11th, having been in St Peter's and on my feet f
a.m. until 2.15 p.m. Lest later paragraphs shou
wrong impression, I must state at the start th
never been more deeply moved in my fifty-thr
The opening ceremony of the Second Vatican
was thrilling; the highlight for me, the singin
litany of the saints.

It was glorious to hear the names of the
martyrs, doctors ringing round the great basili
Church of the twentieth century invoked th
Some three thousand bishops made the respon
a gusto which brought tears even to my ha
eyes. One was moved to add one or two feeble "
us-s" from a perch high above the nave.

The four or five days before the Council pa
most journalists and radio commentators, in hun
exact and stable information about the Council
plans. His Holiness said in his address this morn
the news of the Council was first announced in
1959. Well, there we were on October 10th,
much confusion and with few certain facts.

Thus there was a great reception for the Pre
Peter's at 4 p.m. on Monday, but no one seeme
responsible and we milled about, a thousand of
delightful but ineffectual way. The only door tl
open to receive us was promptly locked. One m
man, perched high on the top of an enormous

had a thousand reckless journalists of all nations struggling and bumping against its base. The story went round that a radio team had been locked in a room for three hours because a monsignor who had gone to Frascati thoughtlessly pocketed the key.

The search for special passes 'to admit bearer' to the basilica this morning took many of us far afield. It seemed to be siesta, early closing and a holiday of obligation all in one. Offices were locked and one ignorant, but well-intentioned, guide who showed us a side-door into the building eventually brought us to a never-ending passage which might well have taken us all the way to the Isle of Capri.

We retraced our steps as best we could and ended up without passes in a delightful restaurant. The tables were crowded with journalists, officials, even Conciliar Fathers who, knowing Rome, had abandoned the chase. You never heard such laughter from men unprepared for and indifferent to their fate.

This morning I celebrated Mass at 5 o'clock, praying hard and long for the success of the Council, and then walked to St Peter's, arriving at the appointed door at 7.15. Long lines of cars transported the Conciliar Fathers. An enormous car would carry a solitary bishop and behind it would be a whole hierarchy wedged into a shooting brake.

On these great occasions one sees nuns and priests in weird and wonderful apparel, some with monstrances and hearts woven in gold and silver on their breasts. Everyone was in the best of humours and there was an atmosphere of exhilaration which the very long ceremony completely failed to quench. Impossible to describe the glory of St Peter's when first I entered, or the

dazzling uniforms and court dress of the thirty officials in front of whom I had to pass. I may have been the only priest in the whole basilica not wearing a soutane. In my clerical suit, I must have looked like a Protestant observer, and this would account for the courtesy and speed with which they passed me through the throng. Rome, the whole of Rome, was anxious to welcome our separated brethren; odd that an English Jesuit of all people should thus cash in on this ecumenical respect. Don't say 'typical'; I felt quite naked and would have done anything to acquire a tassel or a skirt.

Radio Vatican had its equipment in the balcony of St Longinus, high above the nave. One mounted by a spiral staircase inside a massive pillar: myself too breathless to count after the first few hundred steps.

In a space no larger than the Beauchamp Tower, and much more airless, were wedged fifteen commentators and four electricians for six long hours, not one minute of which was dull. Four booths had been erected for the commentators and we had two television screens. These were essential. While we looked direct on to the papal throne, we could not see the altar on which Cardinal Tisserant was to offer Mass. I could see Cardinal Bea, Cardinal Cushing and Cardinal Godfrey, but had only a glimpse of the serried ranks of bishops, and this by hanging over the parapet at considerable risk. The Premier of Ireland was beneath me and he would hardly have wanted an English Jesuit on his head.

We worked in teams. Three of us who were responsible for the African commentary in English, French and Swahili, stood crouched around our microphone and swopped places in strict rotation and without a sound. In the next booth were the Eastern Europeans, next the Spaniards and South Americans, with Radio Eireann in all its glory at the end. Each of us sweated profusely, weighed down as we were with field glasses, cameras, books and notes.

At no moment were we exactly certain what would happen next. The TV commentators suffered a still more tricky assignment in a crypt beneath the altar, for they did not know as they began a sentence what shot would appear next upon the screen. Further, they were standing, touching each other, for six hours, speaking in six different languages.

I watched His Holiness the Pope for six hours with increasing admiration and astonishment. The centre of one of the most beautiful displays ever staged in any city, he seemed inexhaustible and completely at his ease. When he prayed, he prayed with all his heart and with no trace of tension or distraction and, yet, in the very next moment, he would be smiling and gesticulating with great vivacity. When the Cardinals came up to pay their homage, he chatted with each personally and with no formality. Once or twice he even called back a Cardinal for a further few remarks. An octogenarian, he gave his striking address in Latin in a firm and resonant voice. After six hours he looked as fresh and happy as when he had first appeared.

After six hours and when the Pope had gone, I came down from my perch above the altar to look for lunch. At the door of St Peter's, and with thousands of others, I was caught by the stream of mitred bishops pouring out of the central doors. It was bewildering to see bishops at two a penny, their mitres at rakish angles, and a look of liturgical satiation in their eyes. The very number of mitres made one dizzy as when the sun hits the eyes of a motorist driving through a long avenue of trees. We must have stood for half an hour in the porch. It was as though Hollywood had been shooting Van Eyck's famous picture of heaven and the actors were now breaking off for lunch.

One last backward glance into the basilica to note the dazzling effects. I saw a magnificent guard in a field-marshal's uniform chasing three nuns from the steps leading to the Papal throne. O Roma Felix! Amen.

PUTTING THE BISHOPS IN THE PICTURE

Scene One

IT is easy to order photographs in Rome. You just look through the thousands of groups of Conciliar Fathers, make your choice, place your order, pay your money and claim your receipt. I ordered a group of five English bishops in a minute and a half.

Getting your copy may, however, take longer, as I discovered on the following day. My receipt, when presented, caused considerable trouble, much whispering and consultation, followed by an unavailing search. It was generally agreed that Enrico would have found it in a moment but Enrico, alas, was now in Livorno visiting his parents' grave.

I was invited to present myself at the Centro Fotografico, elsewhere in the town. Four eager helpers rattled off the directions; I must cross the Piazza Sisto Quinto, cut down the Viale di Pio Decimo, turn into the Via di Papa Onorio Terzo and then keep straight on. "You can't miss it," they said in cheerful Italian. One had met the same phrase and the same optimism in Spain, England, Germany and France.

8

Scene Two

Noting my hesitation, a young man took me to the door of the shop to explain. I was to take the *prima a destra*, then the *seconda a sinistra* and go right ahead. The signpost across the road said 'Napoli', but I put my trust in God and took a breath. I owed it to the English bishops and must not fail!

At the *prima a destra*, I fell in with a Japanese bishop, small, friendly, enigmatic, as puzzled by the Roman traffic as I was myself. After three weeks in Rome—and who can blame him—his only word in any European language was 'No'. Happily he did not need to explain his present mission, for the receipt in his hand was similar to my own. Together and smiling we went, *prima a destra* and *seconda a sinistra*, to end in a cul-de-sac called after a great Renaissance Pope. Our destination was now obvious for the only shop in sight bore the illuminated sign 'Centro Fotografico' with a sub-heading *'Fotografia Istantanea'* which, at the time, sounded encouraging though I now know that it meant something else.

Scene Three

A small woman in a red jumper stood behind the counter, up to her eyes in episcopal photographs of every sort. Bishops in mitres, copes, soutanes or mufti lay upside down on the counter and on all the shelves behind her back. To the left stood an impressive pile of envelopes.

Gestures come easily in Rome, and to her gesture of welcome and enquiry I made one worthy of a Borgia to indicate that the bishop should go first. He said "No," for he had nothing else to say. She, without hesitation, grabbed his ticket, slapped it on the counter, studied it for seconds, and then, pulling the envelopes towards her, began searching through the pile. She talked to herself and it became clear in a moment that her teeth were first designed for another mouth.

She had covered two hundred envelopes when the phone rang. Dropping the pile, she darted behind the scenes. For ten minutes we heard no more than *"Si-si-si"*: an occasional *"Non ho capito,"* with the archangels Michael, Gabriel and Raphael squashed in between. The Japanese bishop said "No" and slipped into a trance.

Scene Four

When the woman returned, a little flustered, she resumed her counting from the top. She was under pressure now. Other customers had arrived, a fierce-looking man with a camera, who looked American but spoke only German, a German-looking bishop who spoke only American, and three nuns who said nothing but produced a collection box. Three young seminarians peeped in, saw the two bishops and popped out.

The fierce-looking man announced in broken Italian that the Japanese camera which he had bought from her yesterday simply did not work. To emphasize the point, he slapped the camera with so much vigour that two or three vital parts fell out.

The Japanese bishop came out of his trance to say "No." The red-jumpered lady abandoned the envelopes to stand back, wringing her hands. She announced dramatically that her son had gone to God, her husband to Livorno, her daughter to the dogs—the Italian phrase is more expressive—and that, really, she could not run the shop single-handed, General Council or not.

This over, she snatched the pile of envelopes and started again from the top. Two unusual men, Eugenio and Demostene, now appeared behind the counter to encourage the search while picking their teeth. Meanwhile an Italian friar sidled up to me and, in perfect English, asked after the Archbishop of Canterbury. When the Japanese bishop said "No" for me, the friar replied "By Jove" and sidled away.

Scene Five

Another ten minutes had passed before, finally, with a good deal of helpful comment from Eugenio and Demostene, the wanted envelope was at last revealed. We stood round cheering, congratulating, praying, as the Japanese bishop opened the flap to produce his prize. Something had gone wrong. The photograph when produced was of a gloriously apparelled archimandrite, kindly, but possibly not even in union with Rome. Demostene roared with harmless laughter while Eugenio tried to persuade the Japanese bishop that the photograph was the living image of himself. The Japanese bishop said "No" twice and very quickly, for once meaning exactly what he said.

Scene Six

At this stage of the crisis entered a cleric whom I took to be a Jesuit—he carried a breviary, an umbrella and a round, dilapidated hat. Being a Dutchman, he could speak five languages, not one of them Japanese. I guessed that he must be a Jesuit because he made himself all things to all men and took in the situation at a glance. He inspected the broken camera, asked me in perfect English about Coventry Cathedral, with special reference to the stained glass. He understood in a flash the tragedy of the archimandrite and took the offending photograph from the Japanese bishop's trembling hand.

The red-jumpered lady answered *"Non ho capito"* when he addressed her in Italian, followed by German, French and modern Greek. She announced that we would all have to wait until her husband came home from Livorno, where he was rightly visiting his dear parents' grave. Eugenio and Demostene, she said, were only taxi-drivers, off duty, and could hardly be expected to recognize all the bishops of the one and holy Catholic Church. She shed a few tears after this and, to end all discussion, put her hand to her mouth to remove her teeth.

Scene Seven

Spontaneously and to lessen the tension we all then kissed the Japanese bishop's ring. The Dutch Jesuit—I am only guessing—was now mending the Japanese camera, whose furious owner was arguing with Eugenio about football, while Demostene, tooth-picking over, rummaged through the pile of envelopes in a casual and half-hearted way. Nevertheless, he it was who suddenly produced my photograph of the group of English bishops from an envelope marked in pencil 'Los Angeles'. I prayed to St Gregory the Great. The red-jumpered lady resumed her teeth to declare that had Enrico returned from Livorno he would have found the photograph in half the time. The Japanese bishop joined Demostene in saying "No."

The 'Fotografia Istantanea' had now taken me forty minutes and I was prepared to go. The Dutch Jesuit had mended the camera in ten. Only the Japanese bishop was unhappy, and as he could say little or nothing about it, he looked like being thrown to the wolves. He utterly refused, even for the sake of Christian unity, to accept the archimandrite as himself.

Scene Eight

The Dutch Jesuit had just drawn a deep breath to try again in Latin when the door of the shop flew open with a bang. Was Enrico back from Livorno at last? Not a bit of it! Framed in the door stood the gloriously apparelled archimandrite, obviously furious and with a photograph and envelope in his hand. After the first moment of shock, I piously hoped that he would denounce us all in white Ruthenian or in some other rich, Middle-Eastern tongue. Instead, he banged down the photograph on the counter and declared in a very broad Boston accent, "Say, who do you guys think I am?"

The Japanese bishop relaxed at this—he had not wasted the years of American occupation—and, in a Texan drawl, he said something which sounded like "Hi yah, Babe."

The spirit of reunion now triumphed as West, East and farther East fell into each other's arms.

When the red-jumpered lady announced that the Japanese bishop owed her one hundred and thirty lire, the Dutch Jesuit in a twinkle produced the exact change.

PAVEMENT THEOLOGY

No matter what is happening or not happening inside St Peter's, the café theologians seek no respite, know no pause. There they sit at the little tables, sipping coffee, sifting gossip, rushing to the Press Office to phone.

One of them dined last night with an American bishop, two had a 'heart to heart' with a Council theologian, a third was told this, that, and the other by a monsignor whose lips were sealed three weeks ago.

The theology of the pavement is discussed in any language but normally with one small table to each language group. The barbarians from the North rarely develop their thesis with Italians present, for it is of Italians that they hope to speak. They are not for Italy or against Italy, but Italy is at the very centre of their thoughts.

First item on the agenda is the secrecy of the Council which the Italians do not keep. Wise old commentators point out that secrecy in Rome means something very different to secrecy in other places, that the Church is very clever, and that little news gets out despite a lot of talk. The young and the brash complain that Italian newspapers carried the names of the commissions twenty-four hours before these were announced. In an awkward pause a wise old commentator declares blandly, "It seems to me that *Time Magazine* has all the secrets and is running the flipping Church!"

Some pavement theologians are optimistic, some are gloomy, the majority just want something to happen soon. All are united in common respect and affection for His Holiness the Pope. All agree that the Council is running smoothly, but the gloomy ones always add, "You wait!"

Many repeat with glee that things have not yet started moving but that the first signs of revolution are at hand. Why, only yesterday the African bishops met together, and in secret, for the very first time. On the day before, a Dutch bishop from the East criticized the use of Latin, while a Copt, at a private Press conference run by a religious order, said that the Roman liturgy must have no monopoly in a Universal Church. "There you are, the Italian influence again," cries a frantic cleric, sipping his campari in true Roman style.

There is evidence enough, some think, that the system of Church government is changing and that, after the Council, Rome will never be quite the same again. The wise old commentators say that they heard all this when Pope Pius IX was dying, that Rome never changes and must always be the same. One wheezy old man declares that if Rome changes, the world is finished, and that the greatest mistake made by the Popes since the Reformation was when Pius XI bought a car. "An Italian model," said a young man slickly, and half the people round the table laugh.

The pavement theologians feel and express that sense of anxiety, intangible, terrifying, half amusing, which pervades Rome in our modern times. They compare it on a grander scale to Barchester in Dr Proudie's day. The Pope, they admit, stands far above this curious, impersonal atmosphere of censure and restriction, summed up by the café theologians in the personal pronoun 'they'.

'They' do not approve of Hans Kung's little book; 'they' dislike Cardinal Bea's approach to the non-Catholic Churches; 'they' are sniping at the Biblicum.

Do 'they' exist? The pavement theologians certainly think so, but quite different names appear in their several lists.

One wise old commentator, discussing this fear, remarks, laughing, "But don't we all have just the same at home? Don't we also use 'they' of the Government, the Civil Service, even our local hierarchy?" The brash young theologians will not have it, they think that Italy is different, that in Rome we see a mysterious power, an ecclesiastical civil service never answerable in public to Parliament or Press.

Answers a wise old commentator, "All Europe was monarchical a century ago. Now the papacy is the only monarchy left and personally I like it, I find it far more intelligent and friendly than the L.C.C."

The pavement theologians go on for hours and get nowhere; as there is no solution, they can always start again next day. But all their eyes are on the Council just the same. The Conciliar Fathers have made a great impression, free as they seem to be of this civil service taint. Many come from distant countries, look normal, move with an athletic gait. Said a brash young journalist, "Wait till the Americans, Australians, Africans replace the Italians in the Curia." There were tears in the rheumy eyes of a wise old commentator as he answered, "Yes, just you wait."

The pavement theologians ate their own words on one splendid occasion when the Vatican Press Office transported us all to Castel Gandolfo by private bus. All the way there, the conversation turned on the dark and hidden power of the Italian monsignori, so much at variance with the universal charity of the Pope. "Why," said some, as they sat down, two hundred strong, to a slap-up dinner, "only the Holy Father would have thought of this."

A glorious Italian dignitary chose that very moment to make an announcement. "Gentlemen," he said, "with your permission, we will now all be photographed together. My friends in Italian Tourism stood us this meal."

The pavement theologians, brash young journalists, wise old commentators, looked at one another; each was thinking, "You see what I mean."

PRESS CONFERENCE

THE fact must be faced at once that the Church was not established to provide what the journalists call 'news'. The discussions of the General Council afford few headlines and the tempo of debate cannot be speeded because newspapers in Washington or London may be going to press. The journalists marking time in the Roman hotels at this present moment nurse a sense of grievance, for they were wrongly led to expect sensations not catered for in the Apostles' Creed. As an Irish pressman said to me this morning, outside the Press Office, "I do not like even to say it, but if the Sistine chapel caught fire, it would be a lot easier for us all."

One sees today in Conciliar Rome a mingling of oil and water, no more successful in the Press Office than in the liturgy of the baptismal font. In this life at any rate the two will never mix. Rome is Rome but the slick clerical executives from the newer countries have tried to introduce a business efficiency in a body which is not a business at all. All the paraphernalia is there, the long line of telephones presided over by courteous and competent Italian women, stacks of international papers, the ticker tape with its last-minute information, the electric typewriters in the service of any journalist who has anything to type. But who has? After a three-hour session of the Council, some twenty-three Fathers have spoken but their speeches in Latin were prepared several days ahead. It is most unlikely that any of the Fathers will say anything sensational, anything newsy, which will help the poor journalists in any way. Should any young bishop recklessly produce a headline, the secrecy imposed on the Fathers would check its publication for many days.

This shortage of news, which might have been foreseen, has now led to improvisations so that the journalists may seem to be busy without hustling the Church.

Journalists all the world over seem to know by instinct when news is going to break. The Council Press Office, with little or no news at its disposal, yet manages the motions which will bring the journalists out of bed. A whisper goes round, groups talk in the street, an air of excitement in the piazza suggests to those who earn their living by writing that a body has been found. The hall of the Press Office fills up rapidly and one can see late-comers racing down the road.

There are, of course, the hardy annuals who sit in the

office night and day. A tall priest with a red beard way-lays the innocent to tell them the details of a conference which he attended in Damascus in 1948. A wizen journalist of no beliefs permanently occupies a table to do all the crossword competitions in the French, German, American and Spanish press. Two American nuns seem to use the press room to write endless postcards to the friends back home. These are the regulars who gladden the hearts of the officials who twiddle their thumbs behind the imposing, central desk.

When the rumour gets round that important news is certainly expected, the regulars are joined by more casual friends. The nuns come first to park their umbrellas, take out their notebooks and many coloured pencils, that they may not miss a word when the Vatican speaks. Next, fierce-looking friars, clerics, archimandrites, two or three with radio sets about their persons, all very determined to be up-to-date. American journalists arrive with flashy cameras and zip notebooks to stand about and swap asides. The hard-boiled reporters are always last for they have been attending conferences since they left college thirty years ago. These expect very little, have probably written their accounts already and have come because, in Rome, you never know.

The Press Office officials are clever enough to keep us waiting for those extra ten minutes which will bring excitement to the boil. Rumours which started with a modest dispute in the Council about Eastern liturgies now have it for certain that an Armenian patriarch has challenged a Spaniard to a duel.

Enter boys in uniform with the cross keys on their lapels and bundles of papers in their arms. The nuns in front are already writing, bulbs flash in various parts of the hall. The demand for silence spreads backwards and the unbeliever doing the crossword competitions closes his paper and yawns. One can see that the news, this time, is really important, for a monsignor, flanked by Press officials, is at the desk in the centre of the hall. It is announced that the news will be given in six languages, after which questions may be asked.

When the news is given, we learn that a special Mass will be said for the Council journalists at the Church of the Sapienza, next Sunday, and that Cardinal Bambi will preach.

The reaction of the journalists is immediate and always much the same. There is the "Well, that's that" group, who shrug their shoulders and retire to the Corso for a drink. Another set also want a drink but these are more ecclesiastically minded, they see in the selection of Cardinal Bambi a poke in the eye for the Milanese clique. They retire to a café near the Press Office and, over three camparis apiece, argue about Italian intrigues. The nuns note the time of the Mass so that they may tell Reverend Mother; the American journalists photograph the nuns as they write. Two clerics race away to inform Vatican Radio and the *Osservatore Romano*, both of whom will want to comment on this gem.

Within an hour and working furiously, six learned Jesuits have prepared a duplicated script. They set out the history of the Sapienza since the days when Rome was sacked by Attila and details of the life of Cardinal Bambi since he left his mother's knee. Hard-working seminarians translate all this into six languages while the barebones of the statement are chalked up in Arabic on the central notice board. The devoted staff man the central desk of the Press Office; the history of the

Sapienza will be available to journalists till 10 p.m. for no charge.

Yet tomorrow morning the Press of the world will carry columns of facts about the Council, and the bishops going to the Council will smile knowingly. Rome has made a courteous gesture towards Fleet Street and while Cardinal Bambi prepares next Sunday's sermon, the Council continues peacefully on its way.

DEATH COMES TO THE
ARCHBISHOP

AT the start of the General Council, few people were thinking about death. True, many of the bishops were old and frail but, as they filed into St Peter's in their mitred thousands, they seemed to share the permanence of the immortal Church. We must all die one day, but surely not while the Council is on.

Archbishop Chichester, old, stout and very distinguished, survived the long opening ceremonial with all the vitality of the young of heart. Along with the other bishops he had sunk his own individual greatness to become just one of the thousands who made up the General Council of the Church. The Council was gloriously impersonal and each bishop found it a deep, spiritual honour to become one of a vast, international throng.

Archbishop Chichester was probably less well known in Rome than most other bishops; a retired missionary bishop in poor health and over eighty cannot so easily make friends. He was not Roman trained, no writer or scholar, and his achievements in a new country were not so well known in the old world. After his death, it took some time to identify his among the photographs taken on the opening day. He was barely a name in the Rome of the Council, though a famous man at home. The humility of the General Council was impressive and he, of all people, would have wished it so.

At the time of his death, few of the bishops standing around him knew who he was. There were more than two thousand in choir dress making their way to St

Peter's and, when he collapsed, he was carried to an annexe and then to the hospital by the First Aid staff. Few of the bishops knew who had been taken ill, but one, Archbishop Heenan, wrote to me later, "I was quite near to dear old Archbishop Chichester when he fell."

It was not until the end of the conventual Mass which began each session that the news of his death was announced. The bishops of the world rose to say the *De Profundis* for him, and his colleagues from Central Africa whispered to one another, still not certain that they could trust their own ears.

To me it seemed that the greatness of the General Council was brought home vividly with this sudden death. Had he not died, Archbishop Chichester would have returned home after the Council almost unnoticed, probably without having spoken a word. His Latin was atrocious, a subject of fun earlier in his life. He was no more than a competent theologian and of a generation long since out of date. Yet he had been a giant of a man and a very great archbishop, similar in many ways to the other great men who now moved about the city, humble and unidentified. The Council was filled with bishops of deep wisdom and experience, but this fact was first underlined when Archbishop Chichester died.

How quickly the news of his death leaked out! Within half an hour it was widely known that a bishop had died at the very door of the Council, and though his name was sadly massacred by the Italians, stories of his achievements and of his greatness were soon passing round the town. Conciliar impersonality thawed at once and he was called by his international nickname 'Chic'. Friends stood in groups to talk about him and one heard on all sides the recitation of the quips and jokes, mannerisms, courtesies and achievements which had earned him a truly Churchillian reputation in Central Africa.

That same evening on Vatican Radio, Bishop Lamont, an Irish Carmelite bishop from Umtali, had this to say :

"Aston Ignatius Chichester, S.J., titular Archbishop of Velebusdus and formerly Archbishop of Salisbury, Southern Rhodesia, had almost reached the main door of St Peter's this morning on his way to attend the General congregation when he slumped to the ground and died.

"No one had probably taken much notice of the venerable old man as he shuffled his way slowly through the colourful throngs of other Council Fathers, up the stone ramp which leads to the great basilica. He probably stopped from time to time, ostensibly to gaze at the sunlit piazza, but, in reality, to gain his breath, and then he would have started off again, on the ramp (he did not like steps), until he came opposite the majestic façade. Bishops from every nation under the sun stood in groups about the great columns, enjoying a last-minute chat before the day's proceedings began inside. Archbishop Chichester, with his customary polite bow of the head, would have greeted them. Only four more steps to go. He must be on time. He was ever scrupulously punctual and this was no ordinary occasion. The Holy Father's orders were for nine o'clock and he would be there. But it was to be otherwise, for, on the steps of St Peter's in Rome, God called him.

"This was no ordinary man. This was a man of tremendous achievement, of immense spiritual stature, of quite remarkable character. The best blood of old Catholic England ran in his veins. He had been Rector of one of England's greatest Catholic public schools, and when, from its urbane and scholarly atmosphere, his superiors suddenly sent him as a missionary priest to Southern Rhodesia, there must have been many who wondered if the Jesuits knew what they were doing. Obviously they did, for from the moment, two years later, in 1931 when he was appointed first Vicar Apostolic of Salisbury, the Church in Southern Rhodesia really began to flourish. When he resigned in 1957 the hierarchy had already been established, the Catholic population more than doubled, four other ecclesiastical jurisdictions set up, a local clergy ordained and a flourishing congregation of African Sisters brought into existence. Archbishop Chichester laid well and surely the foundations of the Church in British Central Africa and the great edifice which he dreamed of is still steadily rising. This, briefly, is his achievement.

"He was a man of immense spiritual stature. 'Do you think this will please Our Lord?', 'Do you think that people will love God more if I do it this way?' These were the criteria which guided his every action. He was incredibly humble. 'Sorry, old chap,' he would write to the most junior of his priests, 'perhaps you were right after all. I have been thinking about it.' Or he wrote after receiving an unkind letter, 'Dear Mr or Mrs So-and-So; in order that neither you nor I should love God the less, may I thank you for your recent letter.' And again, 'Of course I cannot possibly agree with old Smith or Jones (or whoever it might be) but if he believes the silly things he says, he has the right to say them.'

"How he loved the Holy See and, with what particular regard, he reverenced the present Holy Father. 'He is a decent, respectable age, you know, not like you young chaps!' The Archbishop himself was eighty-three.

"He longed for a Council and said to me, years ago,

that he hoped that he would live to attend one. Not that he particularly thought that the Church required a Council. He felt in his heart the perennial stability and the imperishable youth of the Church, was constantly conscious of its divine origins, wanted to feel its majestic power pulsating through every sphere of human activity. Had the Holy Father asked him to come on his bare knees from Southern Rhodesia to Rome, he would have obeyed promptly, unquestioningly, joyfully.

"What more fitting death than his, obeying the command of his beloved Pope, before the very tomb of St Peter, Prince of the Apostles, and with all the bishops of the world to pray for his soul. I can almost hear his ringing tones and merry chuckle, 'Well, chaps, you have all got to go through it one day and, I dare say, you will just about make it; you must admit that I did it decently.'"

The story and example of Archbishop Chichester was still more gloriously repeated two months after the first session of the Council was complete.

At the funeral in Westminster Cathedral, Archbishop Heenan told of Cardinal Godfrey that His Eminence had known from the start of the session that he was dying of an incurable disease. None of us who saw him ever guessed; not even the English bishops who lived with him for two months in the Venerable English College had any idea that the Cardinal was mortally ill. He attended the Council regularly, spoke frequently, entertained guests, supported all manner of outside activities but, out of sympathy for his colleagues, kept his secret to himself. As soon as the Council was over and he was back in London, Cardinal Godfrey retired and was not seen in public again.

BISHOP ON THE BUS

THE Council has tackled many testing problems, but not that of how to take a bishop on a bus.

My friends just said, "Be a help and take His Excellency to the meeting, will you?"; and the bishop added, as I was phoning for a taxi, "I think we ought to go by bus!"

Now Roman buses are bad enough when you have only your own salvation to consider; a bishop is a marked man both in this world and in the next. I tried the taxi gambit again but His Excellency was determined. "I owe it to my dear mother," he said.

We crossed the Tiber to a bus stop just outside the Florentine Church. His Excellency was showing a glint of a ring and a very small dab of purple, token emblems of his high estate. I toyed with the thought of asking him to approach the bus backwards, for, in the Roman rush hour, danger threatens mainly from the rear. A purple stock is seen too late to effect more than a firm purpose of amendment; if he turned round, it might deliver us from evil. Amen.

His Excellency was far too quick for me. He crossed the road while I was dithering and took up his position in the loose scrum of Romans waiting for the bus to come. His Excellency smiled at them affably, trying to look a man among men. I switched on my Bakerloo expression, hoping to introduce a touch of British class distinction to an otherwise undistinguished face.

The men prowling on the pavement saw the bishop and immediately stood back a pace. Mixing their reverence with Roman cunning, they saw a better chance of winning by taking a flying leap from the bishop's flank. No Italian would push a bishop but, by thus standing back a bit and sideways, they would be on the bus before him without incurring any censure from the Church.

The women in the crowd were more submissive. They had all made their Easter duties, had their umbrellas at the ready and, in helping the bishop forward, would themselves reach the bus before the men. So the women stood in a solid mass behind the bishop while the men went foraging on the wings. The very strategy used by Napoleon at Waterloo or Prince Rupert at Naseby was being mounted in a Roman street.

I could only pray. The bus which pulled up was already crowded, and one heard the crack of bones and the sound of tearing garments as those, so fated, struggled to alight. His Excellency's purple had a profound, almost shattering effect. No Italian, good or bad, will leap from a bus into the arms of a bishop, so each new combatant, shying at the purple, made a snap decision and leapt to one side. Thus was the flanking movement of the men on the kerb effectively blocked. The women in the centre raised their umbrellas and pushed together. I watched with awe as His Excellency moved forward as though raised by unseen hands.

The Holy Spirit was with His Church, thought I; the Red Sea had once more parted and the elect of the Lord was almost home and dry.

His Excellency moved slowly forward, helped by the steady pressure from behind. The liturgy calls women the weaker sex but I can't see why. He had one foot on the step of the bus when a diversion checked him; he and I heard his name shouted from the back of the crowd. Staring sideways, I saw a group of bedraggled pilgrims fighting to reach the bishop's side. There were four women in the party, all of them made in Britain, and two nuns who had learned to use their elbows in that modest but effective British way.

In the Rome of Diocletian they would all have died a martyr's death. Today Rome does not kill its Christians but it does its best. Had I been a bishop, I would have paid no heed to those cries of welcome and affection; this, among other reasons, explains why I have remained a simple priest.

His Excellency knew at once the voice of his sheep. He switched on his pastoral smile to greet these loving children, quite indifferent to the savage words of the bus conductor who was breathing fire from the window of his little cab.

The pilgrims, kicking the devout shins behind them, knelt on at least one knee to kiss his ring. I caught casual snippets of greeting and much high-pitched laughter, "Lourdes 1960—Was it?—My Lord, don't you remember Mary?—Yes, the one who fell off the pilgrims' train!"

You who know Rome will guess that the citizens of Europe's proudest city were not disposed to hear all the details of poor Mary's fall from grace. Swirling round His Excellency, men and women met in deadly conflict, pushing and shoving each other through the narrow aperture. His Excellency first turned, undaunted, to introduce me and, next, turned back to find his friends. The pilgrims had gone as well. I could see them waving frantically from the rear window, while Mary looked like adding to her repertoire by now falling off the bus. Theirs, I felt, had been one of the shabbiest of tricks. As the ladened bus turned slowly into the *Corso Vittorio Emmanuele*, I was sad to see that Mary had not yet broken her neck.

We stood alone, the bishop and I, in the deserted street. "Taxi?" I queried, and His Excellency did not answer at once. He could square his mother later; in the present, a Roman taxi was gliding by. For in the Rome of the General Council, each bus has a taxi just behind it, cruising gently like a seagull waiting for the bits.

HORATIUS HOLDS THE BRIDGE

THEY said to me, "If you *must* walk along the Tiber, turn left and go down the steps. The upper embankment is far too noisy but you will sense our history if you stroll by the Tiber's very brink. You English, God bless you, are hopelessly sentimental; we Romans are hard-boiled but suitably impressed!"

I went down the steps. Not only could I sense Roman history, I could smell it, and as I picked my way gingerly by the turgid, coffee-coloured water I lowered my eyes respectfully to pass two dead cats. Yet there was a thrill in pacing by the Tiber as Paul, Clement, Linus and Cletus had done so many centuries ago. The setting moved me to find my breviary. With the corpses behind me in the distance, I recited the *Magnificat*.

One's soul may magnify the Lord in most situations, but it is not so easy when a joker from the upper embankment tips an old mattress and other bedding at your feet. Linus and Cletus might have carried on, for they were Roman; my mind wandered away. I thought how hard it would be to tip bedding into the Thames at Chelsea without attracting the loving attention of our wonderful police. There were no police by the Tiber and never would be unless some other joker threw them in. Dead cats were there, the spirit of Linus and Cletus, much secondhand bedding, plus Horatius guarding the bridge.

I scarcely noticed Horatius until I tripped on two rusty cables which were holding his crazy craft to the bank. He was dressed like a pirate and wore golden earrings; I doubt if he had shaved since the consulate of Cicero. Friends have since guessed that he was either scavenger or gipsy, they are certain that he must have been a wicked fellow to be avoided at all costs. They are sure that he was not a fisherman, for any fisherman landing a fish from that part of the Tiber would certainly die of fright.

I will never know what Horatius was doing or why he stood balancing in his boat. He seemed to me to be in constant danger as his craft swayed viciously, caught in the current from the bridge. A stout old man, he was wearing a striped rugger jersey which revealed the mass of hair on his chest.

Frankly, I loved Horatius at first sight. He had a naughty twinkle in his eyes and though he might have cut your throat for twopence, I knew that he would never hurt an Englishman or a child.

Conversation was sadly restricted by the language problem, for I spoke guide-book Italian while Horatius' English had both a grammar and pronunciation of its own. I could laugh to fill in the pauses, Horatius had a wealth of Italian gestures. He had only to spit into the Tiber to reveal his very soul.

We opened conventionally and I could see that Horatius was a little puzzled by my clerical suit. He did not look a church-goer but, like all Italians, he wanted a priest to look a priest.

Me. "Non parlo Italiano."

He. "I speaka well the Engleesh."

Me. "Bene; Bene."

He. "You think?"

Me. "Yes."

There was a pause for laughter and Horatius re-arranged his feet in the boat.

He. "Protestante?"

Me. "Catolico."

Horatius said "Bene, Bene" but he spat into the Tiber with disappointment and contempt. With his thumb towards the Vatican, he enquired without words whether I was part of the General Council? When I nodded, Horatius spat again. He certainly did not seem too keen on the Council but he lacked the vocabulary to express his discontent.

To ease his soul, I then started in the standard, tourist phrases to say how happy I was to be in so lovely a city as Rome. I stopped dead as I saw his mouth working and guessed that he was going to spit again. Horatius swallowed hastily before asking if I was English or American.

"English," I said.

Horatius looked quite relieved and indicated that he had been in London once to see his daughter, many, many years ago. He suddenly looked wistful, and though I could not follow his mumbled phrases, I gathered that she was dead. He spat with an air of finality as though to drive a host of memories away.

He did not entirely succeed. His next utterance would

34

have puzzled Linus and Cletus almost as much as it astonished me.

Drawing himself to his full height and with the majestic skyline of Eternal Rome behind him, he said, "Elephant and Castle. Lovely, lovely, lovely," and with thumb and forefinger joined in an expressive circle, raised his hand towards the sky.

Now, today, the Tiber is both swift and swollen with the sudden autumn rain. It looks impressive and historic as it swirls across the towpath and races headlong towards the sea. The cats and the mattress may have reached the Mediterranean, but where is Horatius and his little boat? Will he, one day, sail up the Thames to say, "Elephant and Castle. Lovely, lovely, lovely," before spitting with deep affection into London pool?

I now am forced to walk along the upper embankment; it is certainly noisy but also safer, and dead cats look more peaceful from the air. But Horatius said "Arrivederci" and I would run down the steps and wade into the Tiber for the chance of meeting him again.

22nd SUNDAY AFTER PENTECOST

WITH the Council discussing the liturgy and the active participation of the people, it seemed about time for me to take a trip round Rome. We hear such strange things about Rome. Some say that the Romans never go to church, others that they behave disgracefully when they get there, others that the churches are dirty and out of taste. The Gothic fans pour scorn on Roman vestments and the 'Roman' style in architecture is severely criticized. Is the charge proved that only women go to church? I set out to solve these questions to my own satisfaction with an open mind.

It was the 22nd Sunday after Pentecost, a cold and blustering autumn day. One bore in mind, of course, that Rome has six times the number of churches of any other, comparable city and that, while these are in the centre, many people now live on the fringes of the town.

Trastevere, quaint, colourful and lively, afforded a convenient starting-point. I was in luck. At San Crisogono, with ten young Trinitarians in the retro-choir, the priest had reached the blessing of the 10 o'clock Mass. He gave his blessing to a congregation of two hundred, quite as many men as women. Indeed the bulk of the congregation consisted of young families and, as the little ones were frisky, it made it difficult to count.

He, the celebrant, had barely left the altar when the

36

sacristan appeared at the back. With all the skill of a centre-forward, this good man dribbled a roll of red carpet down the central aisle. This he swept with vigour, brushing the dust on to the congregation now arriving for the next Mass. The priest was at the altar, but he went on sweeping; the late-comers jumping the broom to make their seats.

As the priest reached the Epistle, the organ boomed forth with the opening bars of the Wedding March. Bride and bridegroom trod the aisle with parents, aunts and cousins blowing kisses and shaking hands from side to side. We might not do the same in Britain but all here was natural and dignified. The celebrant continued placidly with the Gospel and in due course the happy families settled down. I was a stranger; they were, perhaps, more interested in me than in the bride.

The fine basilica of Santa Maria in Trastevere, just round the corner, also had a congregation of two hundred, mostly men. The celebrant in green vestments and facing the people had completed the consecration, with eight canons behind him in the stalls.

In the middle of the nave, flanked with hundreds of lighted candles, was a morbid catafalque. A black biretta topped the construction, for this was the annual Requiem Mass for the clergy deceased. The living clergy were very much alive and kicking, five priests were hearing confessions and a sixth gave Holy Communion at an altar in the North aisle. (It would certainly have been the North aisle in Gloucester, but the Romans are less fussy about these things.) After the Mass, the celebrant in green, if I remember right, and all the canons, stood for the absolutions round the catafalque. The bulk of the congregation slipped away devoutly, rattling their beads.

Next, to the Corso, which boasts more churches than any other fashionable street in the world. I ran into another bride outside San Carlo in Corso, her family using the façade of the church for their wedding photographs. No one looked or felt self-conscious and the worshippers for the midday Mass shook hands with the wedding group. Mass was just starting. Two hundred were comfortably seated and another hundred were strolling about liturgically with chairs. Up to this moment, and indeed on the whole excursion, I did not see one collection or collecting box.

The Augustinian church opposite was empty, but its next Mass was at 1.15 p.m. San Giacomo, two minutes away, could reckon 150 young men and women who rose for the Gospel as I entered at the back. They all turned round to stare and, thinking that I was a parson, made no effort to impress. One or two were very much in love—I would almost swear that one couple were holding hands during the Gospel reading, but I, as a pop-eyed Englishman looking for scandal, went away deeply moved.

Where the Corso runs into the Piazza del Popolo stand twin churches, looking outside a good deal bigger than they really are. The baroque style is cunning in giving a very false impression of space. In the first, Santa Maria dei Miracoli, a congregation of about three hundred was listening to a sermon, the preacher standing before a microphone, balanced on the communion rails. He spoke quietly and without those baroque gestures so fashionable when I was a boy.

Twenty yards across the street, the church of Santa Maria di Monte Santo was filling up for what is commonly called the artists' Mass. A bishop was in the porch, Mgr Egidio Vagnozzi, Apostolic Delegate to the United States. Even His Excellency had his time cut out to reach the aisle.

Two minute altar boys stood guard at the door to hand out programmes, beautifully produced. We learned that the Vallicelliano choir would sing 'esegue musiche di Palestrina, Animuccia, Strawinsky e Viadana' and that the classical actress, Lia Curci, would read the Epistle and Gospel in Italian. No Roman bus—and this is saying something—was ever as full as this church.

His Excellency vested at the altar in an informal, nonconformist way. The choir struck up a glorious Kyrie but it was, in fact, a low Mass. The actress read the Epistle beautifully but we did not see her; one smiled to recall how English convent schools used also to read the Epistle but were discouraged after a decision from Rome. Only in this church did I come across beggars, gipsy children, who would not take no for an answer and went on pulling at one's arm.

At 12.45 p.m., I crossed the piazza to the great church

39

of Santa Maria del Popolo, famous for its preachers and, on this occasion, packed to the door. Were there eight hundred in the nave alone? My guess is as good as yours. With one leg in the porch and my nose just round the door, I had time to read the notice giving the times of Sunday Masses: 6, 7, 8, 9, 10, 11, 12, 13 and 18.30.

So much for the old city churches, and my pilgrimage ended in the suburbs and with a modern one. My friends assured me that it was dedicated to St Euclid, an unappetizing title for a saint. I discovered later that the piazza was called after the geometrician but that the church was named after the Immaculate Heart of Mary. Here was a gigantic modern church, built in the past ten years by the Claretian Fathers and seating eight hundred, with room for two thousand at a pinch.

I found such a pinch. The congregation was pouring out from the one o'clock Mass. Cars were jammed, drivers swore, policemen whistled and there was a ten-minute wait for anyone so foolish as to want to go inside. I finally went in. The modern, sterilized style seemed chilly and a disappointment after a morning spent in the dark old churches of Rome. It was spotlessly clean, light and airy, with rows of sturdy, polished benches, lacquered candlesticks on the altars and gay mosaics of Our Lady and of the Sacred Heart. We would have been mighty proud of such a church in Britain and one of the Claretians reckoned that eight thousand people came every Sunday to Mass.

Yes, I needed my lunch and a siesta and felt far too tired to visit those churches which were preparing for evening Mass. It just so happened that I had to pass the Florentine Church at the end of the Via Giulia so I visited this as a token for the rest. Believe it or not, I found a sacristan dribbling down the central aisle with a red carpet which he proceeded to brush. Either the Cardinal Protector had visited the church that morning or was expected for evening Mass. I was far too tired to care.

I dreamed of red carpet and Cardinal Protectors that night. Though very confused and not very restful, it was a happy dream.

ON THE TIBER

Scene: A room off the sacristy. Maria, Gondina and Gemma are twisting wire, tearing paper, sewing frantically.

Maria: Don Luigi wants us to black out all the windows of the dome this year. He insists that we have more stars, thousands of them; what's more, they are going to twinkle up to the Epiphany. Raimondo has fitted a scooter engine to the wheel of a pram.

Gondina: Is there a danger of fire with all that straw about?

Maria: Don't be so gloomy! We have not had a fire of any size since 1953.

Gemma: Will Enrico climb the roof again?

Maria: Oh yes, he has quite recovered; besides, it was his own silly fault. I told him not to cross that ledge with yards of heavy curtain in his teeth. Men always know better. He was lucky to escape with broken ribs.

Gemma: Alfredo can help him. He's not much good at heights but he might as well risk something for the *Bambino*. I wouldn't mind having him in hospital for a couple of weeks!

Gondina: We must get a move on with the dresses. Why are you rigging out poor St Joseph in red?

Maria: Why? Because I happen to have an old red petticoat. If he doesn't like it he must lump it as he did on the first Christmas night. I hear that they are having live birds at Santa Anastasia's this year.

Gondina: I wish we could have a couple of real sheep.

Gemma: We'll make a novena to St Agnes; if that fails, Alfredo can go out and steal them. I could do with him in prison for a spell.

Maria: Yes, he ought to risk something for the *Bambino*. In the whole of Italy there must not be a bigger or better crib than ours.

Curtain

CHRISTMAS CRIB

ON THE THAMES

Scene: The priest's sitting-room. The Canon is reading The Tablet *and puffing at his pipe.*

Sacristan: Oh, Canon, about the crib. Same place, I suppose?

Canon (thoughtfully): I think so, I think so. The figures are in the big cupboard with the Paschal candle. Dust them, there's a good fellow.

Sacristan: I've kept all the straw from last year. Someone suggests a small bulb in St Joseph's lantern!

Canon (putting down *The Tablet*): Don't hurry me, George, old man. Come back and ask me again in a fortnight. I'd like to think about that!

Sacristan: Yes, Canon, perhaps it is a bit risky. Anyway, we'd have to ask the Town Council and the Borough Surveyor for a permit and that takes time.

Canon: All right, let's leave it for this year. I don't want any damage. One of the boys smashed an altar card in 1939.

Sacristan: One wonders what boys are coming to these days!

Canon: Anyhow, they didn't have electricity at Bethlehem. George, let us keep to the Gospel story—we're not in Italy!

Curtain

THE FACE OF THE EARTH

THE outsider, studying the General Council from a café where he sips his campari, is aware of a formidable, hidden force which is guiding the Church. Each day its presence is apparent and, as the weeks fly by, it seems to grow.

How analyse this secret power satisfactorily? It could be the silent influence of the Pope, alert, charitable, urgent: or the force of tradition so vital in the private world of the Vatican. One must also reckon the ponderous, scholarly work of the preparatory commissions which produced a syllabus long before the Council commenced. The Council may be moving slowly, but all know precisely the details of each subject to be discussed.

One might have expected that the united earnestness and wisdom of the bishops would gradually exert a mounting pressure even in the natural order, still more in the spiritual sphere.

All these great forces may have coalesced to get the Council moving in President Kennedy's historic phrase. The outsider is not wholly satisfied that all of them added together would prove an adequate explanation of massive developments now taking shape in Rome.

Those not in Rome cannot hope to grasp the initial problems of the Council which no amount of careful preparation could have hoped to solve. Plans for procedure may look well enough on paper but prove wholly inadequate when the vast throng of participants arrive. The Council is enormous, five times as large as the House of Commons, certainly the largest Congress that the world has ever seen. The attendance never dropped below two thousand and was above two thousand five hundred for many weeks.

The Council differs from Parliament in this, that it has no nucleus of experienced members who have been attending for many years. None of the two thousand bishops and Conciliar Fathers, not even the Pope himself, has seen a General Council before. The last General Council, short and hurriedly ended, took place nearly a hundred years ago. Since that time the Church has spread, not just to new countries, but virtually to two or three new continents. Missionary countries are now established and have brought to the Council, not just one or two European missionary bishops, but whole native hierarchies. The consequent confusion at the beginning was very much less than a modest historian might expect. To look back to the days of Oliver Cromwell or to the France of the National Assembly is to grow in astonishment at the success of Rome.

In the opening session in St Peter's, it became very clear that the bishops of the world who look so orderly on paper take on a new and frightening aspect when they file out of St Peter's for half an hour, four abreast.

At the second congregation, when it came to listing the names for the various commissions, the simple task of putting a cross on paper proved too great. Fathers hardly knew each other and were not likely to for many weeks.

When the general debates began, the sheer number of potential speakers put paid to any plan. No one could visualize how any debate would ever stop. As to the length of the Council, the less pessimistic thought in terms of years. One English bishop in a radio talk remarked that while he and his colleagues were now debating the liturgy, it would be their successors who would come to Rome to vote.

The outsider, sipping his second campari, sits amazed at the wisdom which resides in Rome. Where a modern Government would have been forced to impose a guillotine clause amidst shouts of protest, the General Council waited with consummate tact.

It was thought likely that many would want to speak at first for the sake of the records, for it must be a temptation, hard to resist, to speak in a General Council of the Church. Soon there were appeals for shorter speeches, even a quotation from Cicero placed by his colleagues in an offender's place. One bishop remarked that the most powerful weapon for curbing speeches was the look on one's neighbour's face.

This first session has moved very slowly, weaving its rules of procedure as it goes. There has been complete freedom of speech and the only check has been the spirit which binds the Conciliar Fathers to the Church. Bishop Muldoon of Australia quoted in a radio address the opinion expressed to him by a non-Catholic observer who had been astonished at the liberty allowed.

The outsider, sadly sipping the last of his second campari, cannot recall having seen democracy work more smoothly in any modern, democratic state. The Catholic Church is not democratic in any strict, political sense. Yet the results have been more impressive in her Council than in very many parliaments.

In those first few hectic days when bishops were milling about with spectators cheering on the touchline, it seemed certain that the Council, like United Nations, would form itself into national or racial blocks. Indeed the voting for the commissions seemed almost a cross between the Derby and an American Congressional election: there were cheers and boos along the Via della Conciliazoni as though the Republicans or Democrats had lost a place. National hierarchies began to meet in private and monsignori were seen rushing about and peddling lists. Those were the days when bishops and nations carried labels and everyone wanted to look like a liberal.

All this has now ceased. Even on the vexed question of the vernacular on which it was taken for granted that all missionaries would vote against Latin, Conciliar Fathers from all five continents have been found on either side.

The Council is proving classless, raceless, ageless, and this is surely a miracle in the modern world. It is the human instrument of a power unseen, silent, which bloweth where it willeth, which once more will move across the frontiers and renew again the face of the earth.

TOO OLD AT FIFTY

*[Fragment found in a Roman waste-paper basket
and left there]*

While prelates pace the streets each day,
We, lesser fry, prefer to pick
The side-walks which afford a way
Less obvious but just as quick;
So I, by some supernal plan,
Met with my seminarian.

'Twas in San Giacomo's and he
Betrayed his status in his looks.
He sat there, frowning; on his knee
Two leather-bound, scholastic books;
I recognized the pain of one
Whose studies had, that term, begun.

"Young man," said I, "you must not quail,
For you are young and life is gay.
Wisdom and study will prevail,
You'll be a bishop, one fine day.
The Fathers, if you only knew,
Once sat and mugged it up like you."

He thanked me with a boyish smile,
Agreeing that the work was grim.
I knelt to say my prayers awhile,
And, on departing, waved to him.
He, too; I, rooted to the floor,
Gaped at the golden ring he wore!

America

THERE are lovely expressions in every language but none more soothing to the weary pilgrim than "You're welcome" said with an American drawl. The Italians say "Prego," the British "Don't mention" with much the same kindness but without the same effect. "You're welcome" rings round the United States and has served as a signature tune during the General Council, for the Americans drawl the phrase with such genuine feeling, and they mean what they say.

Yes, it is the signature tune for one of the most generous nations in the world. One of the most humble, too, for despite all the tales of American boasting, the Americans in Rome for the General Council have provided a lesson for the Church.

They take it in such good part if they are treated as

49

country cousins, if they are teased about their lack of Latin, their love for gadgets, their youthful enthusiasm for cultural tours. In this their humility is breathtaking; they do not mind appearing as though they were learning from their betters and they rarely quote their massive achievements back home.

Let us face it: for sheer devotion to Our Lord put into practice in every part of a continent as large as Europe, the Catholics of the United States stand unique. Europe has nothing to show them in love for the sacraments, sacrifice for Catholic education, generosity towards the foreign missions, contributions for the upkeep of the Church. They say little about all this. They just drawl "You're welcome," listen humbly to the pitiful boasting of European pigmies and then pile into cars and buses for one more cultural trip.

The United States bishops, bland, hygienic, drip-dry, look almost too clean for the Catholic Church. You could, I believe, pick them without error in any Conciliar identity parade. American bishops talk to anyone, listen to anyone, welcome anyone with Christian kindness as their only end. Their secretaries, standing in groups at street corners, provide the fastest and wittiest wisecracks heard in Rome. In every convent or religious community, male or female, the American contingent is the most kindly, most tolerant, most refreshing to meet. In the Press Office among the journalists, most of all among the telephone operators, frustration fades if you are lucky enough to have an American at the other end. As for the tourists, it takes a party of American sightseers to make you feel how lucky you are to be in Rome.

With rare but obvious exceptions, the American bishops are not Latin scholars, not even authors, orators or journalists. They are deeply Roman but without a mincing and painful veneer. What they never say in public—and only with modesty when they are in private—is that they have never lost the link between clergy and people which, in some other countries, is wearing so very thin. They never say that while priestly vocations are desperately few in some other countries, their American seminaries are splitting at the seams. No, they just say "You're welcome" and send their young men to work for Our Lord without payment in every part of the world.

France

Outside their own great country, it is never easy to find the French. In Rome they do not stand about in groups or gossip at street corners. Where the faith is concerned, the French are not partial to small talk.

When the Conciliar Fathers stream from St Peter's at the close of a meeting, an attitude of schoolboy relaxation after lessons spreads among the Anglo-Saxon groups. Australian bishops have been known to discuss cricket or the Melbourne Cup. Not so the French bishops, who leave the piazza in earnest conversation about some sore, theological point. They may be gay, cynical, even savage, but their moods are built on reason and their minds are probing far ahead. American bishops carry glossy cases, the French write in pencil on the backs of envelopes and will speak for hours without notes.

Few, I think, would dispute the central role played by the French bishops and theologians in the present Council of the Church. From the very start Cardinals Liénart and Tisserant were recognized by the journalists as 'news'. De Lubac, Congar and Daniélou, to mention but three theologians out of fifty, have established the French supremacy in the theological world. There is no single project in the long Conciliar programme on which the French are not expected to take a vigorous line of their own. In ecclesiastical art and architecture, liturgical reform, the study of Sacred Scripture, the French hierarchy is expected to give a determined lead. No rumours run round that the Anglo-Saxon block is taking a line or putting its foot down. Things may be different in the secrecy of the Council, in public everyone expects fireworks from the French.

This quiet, rational power extends down the line from the bishops and theologians, priests and secretaries into the exuberant world of journalists. At the very first Press conference in St Peter's, the journalists of many nations were laughing, jostling, photographing, frantically scribbling notes. At the last moment, a frail, sinister little man of uncertain age crossed the piazza and picked his way up the steps. He looked around with a beady eye, nodded to two or three acquaintances, turned and retired the way he had come. "That is Dubois of the Paris X," said an American journalist, "he knows more about Rome and the Council than the lot of us." Maybe he did. The French papers certainly covered the Council with precision; they were alert, respectful, witty, cynical but always intelligent. It is odd that the nation which filled half the world with sentimental gush about God in the nineteenth century now markets a neatly-packed and dehydrated faith.

The strength of the French in Rome—surely it has always been the historic strength of French soldiers, missionaries, explorers—is a complete indifference to physical comfort and luxury. Whether from asceticism or preoccupation, French bishops and theologians are rarely seen in hotel lounges or at monster meals. While the other Churches are drinking French wine as the French have taught them, the French argue about the Mystical Body while dipping their biscuits into hot milk. They squeeze into pocket cars and some of them look as though they would prefer to arrive at the Council with a beret and a bike. A French bishop with a camera, golf clubs or radio would look very out of place. The French Church is courteous beyond measure, suffering fools gladly for Christ's sake.

On one of the first days of the Council, the English and Australians in Rome were to meet in the Pamphili gardens for a cricket match. Five of us wedged in a car lost our sense of direction, so we stopped to enquire of a bishop who was pacing the Janiculum. His Excellency turned out to be French. He expressed his sorrow with an old-world courtesy but his look of pained amusement made the day for us.

53

England

We English Catholics living in Rome owe a great debt to our non-Catholic friends. They create an interest, offer to us an unusual status, provide for our odd behaviour both explanation and excuse.

As the world grows uniform, intelligent men are attracted by what is different in dress, food, architecture, entertainment, modes of thought. The Protestant Reformation made us different, whether we like it or not. Not only do we drive on the left of the road and spurn the decimal system, but we approach theology in an amateur and mildly non-conformist way. Henry VIII made us naughty, odd and entertaining though, sadly enough, so many of our national idiosyncrasies are now wearing away.

Without the advantages of this non-Catholic background, the English Catholics in Rome for the Council would be swallowed up in the vast, cosmopolitan throng. The great continental blocs of bishops and theologians, the massive achievements of the Church in other places, make all our efforts and successes seem pitifully small. We cannot console ourselves for ever

54

with the reassuring statement that the Catholics of Wigan and St Helens are the best in the world. Despite our virtues and our five or six million Catholics, ours is still a pigmy Church. This was one of the first lessons taught by the Council in Rome.

I found a curious confusion, for while all the other nationalities somehow hoped that the British would look different, our aim since the days of Faber and Manning has been to look as continental as Englishmen ever can. Wiseman and his friends, in trying to make us more Roman, may have also made us more banal. Who can blame them? British insularity in their day was so obnoxious and self-sufficient that they had to start at the beginning and re-fashion the English link with Rome. Has the time now come to reverse the process in the belief that national variations add greater lustre to a Universal Church? To have studied in Rome, to pronounce Latin in a Roman way, to think like the *Osservatore Romano* may once have been achievements to be admired, but do they weaken our genius today? In theology, hagiography, piety, architecture, music, Catholic Action, could imitation be a sign of cowardice rather than of flattery? Where the Germans, the French, the Spaniards have their own distinct lines of thought on theological problems, our reputation at the Council was based on charming but not very theological points. It was widely agreed that ours was the most developed sense of humour and that the Commonwealth Fathers gave an impressive example in waiving their right to speak in the Council when the bishop before them had said what they intended to say. Few other nations liked to forgo a chance to speak.

While we have been looking Romewards for a century, the Catholics of Europe have been gazing fervently towards England and over our heads. Their glance is not directed to St Edmund's, Ware, Heythrop or Blackfriars but to Oxford, Buckingham Palace and Canterbury. Cardinal Manning as a convert played an impressive part in the First Vatican Council and another convert archdeacon of the same calibre would have caused a greater stir today. Newman's giant stature is now widely recognized, Robert Hugh Benson is still remembered, Monsignor Knox might not have liked it but he could almost have stepped into Manning's shoes. It was interesting to note that when Archbishop Heenan wrote about the English Church in the *Osservatore Romano*, His Grace chose for his illustration a fine panoramic view of Oxford, and this immediately gained profound attention from an interested audience. In His Grace's list of famous English writers the majority were converts, while the Abbot of Downside, an Oxford convert, commanded universal respect.

The English Catholic Church has played a quiet, shrewd, observant role in the present session of the Council, while England herself enjoys an unparalleled respect. Sir Alec Guinness commands the awe due to a domestic prelate, Richard Dimbleby would have received ecclesiastical preferment in the good old pre-Reformation days. A Frenchman asked after Dr Fisher, a Belgian quoted Scotland as a wonderful example of tolerance in education, two German theologians pray daily that Newman may soon be canonized. Even the footballer Charles, the idol of Rome and called 'King Charles', brought a reflected sympathy and glamour to the English Church. Non-Catholics in Britain should feel both pleased and flattered: we, who have the faith as well, should be doubly grateful for we could easily enjoy the best of both worlds.

Africa

In Rome today it is an advantage to be black. You look different and are treated with a courtesy not always shown to whites. The world is used to white bishops since the golden days of Fra Angelico. People take them more for granted and they must be exceptionally tall, short, fat, thin, conservative or progressive to become 'news'. Outside the London School of Economics, Africans are still a novelty. In Rome, African students and African bishops gladden all hearts.

At first sight, the Africans in Rome seem a happy, enthusiastic, uninhibited group. You never pass an African priest in the street without a sunny African grin of recognition, returned in our solemn English way by the raising of a non-existent hat.

Everyone in Rome loves the Africans, for they are simple, generous, gentle, boyish and intellectual in a refreshing, non-Thomistic way. To talk with them is to escape into a sunshine free of Bernini, Barberini and the rest.

When one greets an African, one feels that here is a man whom God loves, who loves God, who has everything in common with me without ever having bothered much about the New Westminster Hymnal and Burns and Oates.

Everyone knows—intelligent Africans are very intelligent—that the formation of a stable African community will demand great patience and take many years. The stature of Cardinal Laurian Rugambwa is great in this, for while he personifies the Africa of the future, free of inferiority and western pressure, he is yet fully Roman in its widest and most universal sense.

It would be hard to exaggerate his prestige. Other native African bishops reflect his wisdom when they attempt to follow his lead. Theirs is no easy task. Many of them are fighting on two fronts, against the old colonial paternalism, which now looks so odious, and against that sense of grievance and inferiority which so often dogs the African student at our universities.

One Indian bishop was shocked and surprised at the occasional signs of strident prejudice heard on the Council floor. He wondered if some of the African bishops bore the added burden of what would be said of them at home. One point is certain, that the African bishops are playing a more and more important part in the General Council and that, after their first united meetings here in Rome at the Council, they will go ahead with renewed courage to build a lasting Church. Rome is proving both colourless and classless. Where in other parts of the world the Africans are fighting for recognition, they speak as equals in the Catholic Church.

The Church, if allowed to do so, might still make Africa. It has been a thrilling lesson to both Africans and Europeans that the Catholic Church at its centre stands above racial taboos. When we all sing the Creed together, colour prejudice does not exist. Here surely

Class No.	AUTHOR (Surname first)		
	Bassett, S.J., Bernard		
Accession No.	TITLE		
	Priest in The Piazza		
Date Ordered	Touchline tribute to a Council		
Date Received	Edition or Series		— Volumes
9/03/85			
Dealer	Place and Publisher	Year	List Price
Gift	The Catholic Book Club	1963	Illustrate
No. of Items Ordered	No. of Copies		
Cost	Recommended by	Approved by	
No. List No.	Remarks in	Fund Charged	
		Theology	10252041

is the germ of world government based on concepts which few of the politicians of any colour can understand.

The Council will prove a lasting joy in this. Each African student in the seminary carries a pallium in his briefcase; he has as much chance as any Western colleague of one day exercising the highest powers in the Church.

The heroes of this African evolution are the European missionary bishops and the day of the Lord will be brought much nearer when Christians of every colour recognize this fact. Here are men who left home and country for the sake of Africa. Though their skin remains reasonably white, they carry in their bodies the pricks inflicted by either side. They are martyrs to three causes, for they love Africa, their own country and God.

When the story is told in a thousand years time— perhaps an African Pope will call a General Council at Nairobi—the world will salute the missionary bishops as it hails St Boniface, SS. Cyril and Methodius today. It would be sad if we must wait a thousand years to accept an historic fact.

One final slant. While native African bishops are anti-colonial, the French-speaking group on theological issues remain entirely in line with Metropolitan France. The English-speaking group are far less European in their Catholic thought. This is not surprising, for they learned little theology from Westminster, Washington and Whitehall. In place of this, they have a clear sense of Parliament and procedure which, in the coming years of African development, will stand them in good stead. How fascinating it is to see and to speak to the men who now and in the future will fashion the African expression of the one true faith.

THE COCKTAIL PARTY

THE presence of non-Catholic observers at the Vatican Council at first took many by surprise. Happily, charity was in good supply on both sides of the theological curtain and most people were more anxious about their own behaviour than about the dogmatic eccentricities on the other side. If, later in the session, we took each other more for granted, at the start all were understandably shy.

There was a certain amount of homework to be done. We heard of an Anglican dignitary who was up all night reading a soppy life of St Margaret Mary so that he could chat pleasantly about the Nine First Fridays should the chance arrive. On the other hand an Irish theologian from County Cork was caught with a coloured guide to Ripon Cathedral, while two American prelates memorized the quotations from Jeremy Taylor in their diaries. When the ever-cheerful bishop of the Stand-Off Isles referred to the devil himself as 'our separated brother', many thought that he was going too far. In excuse it was pointed out that His Excellency was himself a convert and that the Episcopalian sense of humour was far more developed than anything out of the Gregorian.

When the bishop's secretary asked me to accompany them to an official cocktail party, I piously demurred. The secretary begged me to be a help—and added, in a whisper which almost dislocated the Roman telephone service, that the observers would be there. He went on to deplore the time that he had wasted in the seminary at Dogma lectures and told me that the bishop, with his feet up, was, at this very moment, reading the life of Pelagius. To my plea that I could not help very much he answered that I was talking nonsense; that, as a Londoner, I would know the difference between Lambeth Palace and Fulham Palace and that reunion might turn eventually on small points like these.

As with all cocktail parties, a great many mature and distinguished people had been squeezed into a very modest room. A Conciliar cocktail party produced the further problem of distinguishing the various styles of ecclesiastical dress. Where, normally, only the ladies wear flowing gowns, here half the men looked like Lawrence of Arabia with or without a rosary round his neck. To Dominicans and Trinitarians were added Fathers of Mercy, Pity, Tenderness and Compassion either straight from the Sahara or from the operating theatre of Dr Kildare. Bishops looked like monsignori,

monsignori very much like bishops and no one knew much about two high personages in ruffs and capes. Nor were the observers dressed very different from the rest. It had been hoped that their dark, clerical suits would preserve some of the austerity of the Reformation and that their conversation would be based on the scriptural Aye and Nay. In fact we lacked such guidance and it was surely a step towards reunion that we all looked very much the same.

Our bishop, hesitant in the hotel and determined to restrict himself to tonic water, now threw off all inhibitions and circulated in a true, ecumenical way. In the cause of reunion he wore the O.B.E., awarded for his work on the foreign missions, and limited his conversation to those simple, homely, non-dogmatic topics which Mormons, Copts and Jacobites would understand. It was hit and miss at first. His Lordship started on the Test Match with an Italian monsignor whose ecumenism hardly went as far as that. Neither the secretary nor I knew the Italian word for Ashes so we all roared with laughter and then went our several ways. Next, we spoke to an American diplomat about the genius of Billy Graham until he disclosed to us that he was a graduate from Immaculata College, Mo.

Waiters moved around, guests twisted themselves sideways; to kiss a bishop's ring was to spill your neighbour's dry martini; there was talk of Billy Graham, Dr Fisher and the Test Match on every side.

I was detained for several minutes singing the praise of Dr Niemoller; meantime His Lordship had wormed his way across the room. He was deep in conversation with an obvious observer, an elegant cleric with an Oxford accent, gold cuff links and a dark, Savile Row suit. They were discussing the founts of revelation as I approached them, both doubling over backwards to see the other's point of view. Both agreed that it was wonderful that the Churches should come together, both turned to ask for tonic water from the waiter passing with a tray. His Lordship went so far as to invite the observer to tea on a later occasion, promising him real tea and not that stuff out of those little American bags. The observer became more and more Oxford, remarking that His Lordship was too, too right.

On our way out, His Lordship was confident that the conversion of England was as good as settled, that the kind of tolerance that he had met this evening would erase the errors of three hundred years in a trice. Even His Lordship's accent had moved towards Oxford and he said "God bless you" to the man who took his tumbler with some of the patronage of the senior Common Room.

"For the love of the Lord, don't tell him," said the secretary to me in the cloakroom, "that fellow he was converting is a Californian Jesuit doing a doctorate at Oxford on marine plants."

I met the marine plant expert on the pavement looking for a car. He, too, thought that the conversion of England would come at any moment; why, he had been talking to an Anglican observer dressed, my dear fellow, just like one of ours. "I could tell at once," he added grandly; "he wore an O.B.E. and talked about the Test Match, but he knew his Pelagius."

HIS EXCELLENCY EATS OUT

THE bishop was lodged in a modest hotel on the fringe of the city; it took physical stamina to get there and great moral courage to come out again. Once home after the morning congregation, His Excellency was tempted to sit still and say his breviary in peace.

Once every week, on Thursday, he turned tourist, for the General Council did not meet on that day. He was ever mindful that he must improve his mind and relax a little while maintaining a dignity proper to the Church. Thus, one could not just drop in at the first restaurant which caught the eye. It might be too luxurious, too fast, too loose, too dirty, and there were, too, the feelings of the other clients to be borne in mind. A boy out with his girl, or a Dominican chatting about Suarez with a Jesuit, would hardly want to sip their ministrone under a prelate's baleful eye.

On the day that we 'did' the forum, it was not so easy to find a place to eat. We condemned the Casa Poppea on account of that lady's goings on with Nero which, the bishop's secretary assured us, would never be recognized in Canon Law. His Excellency agreed and suggested instead a short visit to the church of the Quaranta Corone, and there we prayed for a little space.

We spurned the Lucrezia Borgia for an additional reason; the bishop, gazing at the trifle in the window, noticed two flies which had started their eternal rest. At His Excellency's request, we crossed to the Chiesa dei Due Fratelli and again prayed. The secretary, in an aside which might have carried down the Corso, feared that we would have to be content with Holy Water à la Borghesi unless we were quick. His Excellency pretended not to hear. He was reading in the porch an announcement of a special, super-charged novena which would get you out of Purgatory before you could say 'knife'.

Knife conjured up phantasms of a more worldly sort. Yet we passed La Petacci without batting an eyelid and dropped into the church of Santi Martiri del Seminario to pray for grace. The secretary, more subdued, whispered to me that the only grace he wanted was the grace before meals. He would try to resist but I must not be shocked if I saw him eating the altar cards. He had been on his feet since 6 a.m. with only a bowl of coffee to sustain him and, though he had gained forty-three plenary indulgences, he still felt a gap in his soul.

His Excellency suddenly remembered that there used to be a very nice little place behind the Minerva, to which he had sometimes gone in his seminary days. His Excellency looked right and left over his shoulder before he revealed this fact. He assured us that it was simple and inexpensive, frequented by more broad-minded professors and even by Pope Pius XII in his Capranica days. His Excellency thought that we might, on the way, call in at the Minerva for a little prayer. In fact, when there, he recited the Angelus with us, the secretary at least one invocation ahead. The secretary said that he was feeling so wicked that he dare not look St Catherine of Siena in the face!

Alas, we could not get behind the Minerva, for Mussolini had changed the layout; in place of the restaurant, we found a small forum, full of fragments of the Rome of former days. The secretary said that he would not mind trying a piece of stone column only it looked a little underdone. His Excellency, too, was growing hungry; we passed the Church of San Vapore without going in.

Though our hunger was increasing, our training stood us in good stead. We passed the Trattoria Lollobrigida and the L'Anticlericale with our eyes modestly dipped. His Excellency never looked up but he informed us that the menus in both these places had looked excellent and were very reasonably priced.

It was the bishop's secretary who, next, tapped me on the shoulder and asked me to confirm what he thought he saw. Here was no mirage. Between a tobacconist and a hat shop stood the Ristorante Santa Maria Goretti with a picture of the saint above the doorway and, in the window, an antique paschal candle casting its light on a dish of delicious prawns. "Here," said His Excellency with fervour, "is an answer to all our prayers."

We went in. His Excellency was a little depressed by the sight of so many of his Conciliar colleagues; I think that he had hoped to announce his discovery in the Council coach on the following day. Still, he was not for moving on, not even when the secretary had talked to a waiter and passed on the information that the restaurant was communist owned. The secretary said that

Nenni and Togliatti came regularly on Fridays because the fish was so good. Said His Excellency with vigour, "Well, today is only Thursday so I vote we tuck in."

The proprietor, when he did the rounds, warmly greeted our bishop and was clearly delighted with our heartfelt praise. He told us how much he liked the British and admitted his very great debt to England, for he had first heard of the General Council in London on his summer holidays. In London, too, he had been informed about the saint whose name he was so proud to bear. The very idea of the Ristorante Santa Maria Goretti had come to him in London and he had bought the picture, now over the doorway, at a shop with a strange name, something like *Buongiorno and Oates*.

The proprietor did not want to anticipate the judgment of the Church but he, in private, would always hold it as a miracle the way that his restaurant had flourished in recent weeks. During the Council, the saint had brought him a very much nicer type of client and he was grateful to her for that. He had already put up three candles in her honour and might do something still more generous later on. The beauty of the whole scheme, he explained, warming to his subject, was that he could still revert to his old title and customers at the week-end. The portrait of the saint was movable and Conciliar Fathers, quite understandably, did not dine out at week-ends.

His Excellency, after lunch, suggested a short visit to a church just across the street. The secretary stayed behind to pay the bill. When he caught us up, he informed me that, at week-ends, the restaurant was known as Rosticceria San Lorenzo; in answer to my query he thought that *Rosticceria* was the Italian word for Grill.

HIS EXCELLENCY TIPS THE SCALES

AT the beginning of the Council, there were so many other weighty matters to consider that few had time to fuss about their avoirdupois. One was just careful and hoped that the effects of the delicious *pasta* would be counter-balanced by the fruit.

Only after a full month did the bishop's secretary raise the subject on the phone. He asked quite simply, "How in the heck do I borrow weighing scales and how many flipping kilos are there to a stone?" He is a gentle soul!

I suggested the National Colleges where, no doubt, the scales used by Ullathorne and Manning are still preserved. The secretary was doubtful, reminding me of the twin-headed monster of protocol and prestige. "Why," he said, "we have an American bishop in this hotel with an all-plastic weighing unit made for air travel, but we dare not ask him for fear of offending Commonwealth interests."

The hunt for scales was no more successful than the search for information about stones. Every Italian priest replied, with matching gestures, *"Che cosa è una pietra?"* or words to that effect. One ancient German missionary could confirm that a stone was a standard of measure but his knowledge ended with the priceless detail that he had weighed 11 stone 10 lbs in 1907 on a Bombay weighing machine.

The Contessa was my hope. She, after all, had lived for many years in England and was skilled in simple domestic problems such as this. She laughed encouragingly when I asked her and said that she must run upstairs for her English cookery book. She calmed my apprehensions. It just so happened that she had had to convert lbs into grammes for an Apple Charlotte and had pencilled the required information into the cover of the book.

When she returned, she produced crested notepaper in honour of the bishop and made rapid calculations, whispering to herself.

I threw in His Excellency's weight, as last recorded, and the mixture was allowed to simmer for a while. The Contessa next announced—and she was frowning —that the bishop appeared to weigh forty-three milligrams. "There must be something very wrong with your bishop," she said; "I never make a mistake."

The deadlock was broken only when the Count, her husband, arrived home for lunch. He was a scientist of no small repute and was home from reading a paper on the density of commercial asphalt to an industrial group. He informed us at once that His Excellency should weigh 83·623 (recurring) kilograms and added that it was high time that Britain came over to decimals and to the right side of the road.

How to put our data to the test? His Excellency answered this himself after a Council session while we were wandering around the lovely old church of Santa Maria in Trastevere. His Excellency was admiring a glorious mosaic of flying angels when he turned and declared with vigour, "I must go and be weighed!"

The secretary said at once that only the Aga Khan was weighed in public, but His Excellency brushed this irrelevance aside. He was out of the church and across the road in a flash. Bishops see far more than one imagines and His Excellency must have noticed the sparkling chrome and enamel contraption in a neighbouring bar. The secretary and I anxiously followed, he begging me to guard the right-hand pavement, for the journalists from the English Catholic papers were certain to be snooping about.

The proprietor advanced smiling to greet the bishop and said how pleased and proud he was as a devout Catholic to help like this in the Council of the Church. He also informed us that two famous Cardinals had come to this very shop to be weighed, every fortnight, during their seminary days. With a noble flourish, he bowed the bishop on to the little platform, declaring to all and sundry that this one was 'on the house'.

There was a sudden whirl of wheels, the needles danced on the four dial faces, digits appeared and settled down in the small, central square. There was a very awkward pause. His Excellency, who should have weighed 83.623 (recurring) kilograms, stood in Trastevere at 93 kilograms.

The poor secretary looked dejected, obviously taking the full blame to himself. In watching the Council, he had let the carbo-hydrates take care of themselves. The proprietor was delighted, announcing with gusto that His Excellency had beaten both the famous Cardinals, at least in their seminary days. His Excellency, still on the platform, looked wistful and slightly puzzled for a moment, then, a shy, Sir Alec Guinness expression flitted across his face. He raised both hands slowly and fumbled in the folds of his soutane. Out of a pocket, not without some pulling, His Excellency produced a massive piece of rock.

"I was given this yesterday at the catacomb of St Domitilla," he said.

Wiping his brow on his sleeve, the secretary accepted the souvenir and held it reverently before him as the wheels whirled again. The needles stopped their dancing and, as His Excellency now stood at exactly 83·623 (recurring) kilograms, the world, the Council and the diocese could smile again.

His Excellency alighted from the platform with a joyous little jump. He is a serious man and his next remark was of the kind which he reserves for the Paschal season. "It would seem that it is only St Domitilla who has lost a stone," he said.

ALL SOULS' DAY

November 2nd and, indeed, the week-end following, was given over by Romans to prayers for the dead. In St Mary Major, an enormous catafalque blocked the nave. Each Roman church had a similar elaborate structure, surrounded by candles and with a black cushion on the very top. The same black cushion appears on each coffin during a funeral Mass.

No one seems very certain of the exact purpose and symbolism of this cushion, but it looks very well. They say that it goes back to the days when coronets, helmets, swords and decorations afforded a last glimmer of class distinction to the man or woman lying just beneath. Today no one has such decoration, but everyone gets a cushion on which he can no longer sit.

Masses in St Mary Major were offered throughout the morning and the great basilica was filled with people, many of them men.

In the retro-choir, a Cardinal and four bishops were assisting at the office for the dead. The choir was composed of seminarians who sang with a gusto frowned on at Solesmes. The seminarians looked refreshingly happy for a funeral; some of them were painfully young.

The Campo Santo

It was an unforgettable experience to visit San Lorenzo and the famous cemetery beside it, especially at this particular week-end. How complete is the contrast between this and the celebrated 'Whispering Glades' at Los Angeles so aptly described by Evelyn

Waugh. There was death as the ITV adverts would like to have it, here was life and death in the raw.

I never saw in my life a happier cemetery than this one in Rome. All the world and his wife were there with the children, grandchildren and great-grandchildren, laughing, praying, arranging flowers round the graves. In the centre, a floodlit statue of Our Lord rising in glory radiated hope.

The Campo Santo, with its vaults, mortuary chapels, mausoleums, niches, looks like a miniature town. Indeed some of the tombs appeared more dignified and spacious than the pre-fabs which disgrace our British towns. I preferred this cemetery to parts of Slough!

As night fell and each tomb showed a light before it, the Campo Santo also looked more alive than many towns. In a quiet, residential part stood the Jesuit mausoleum, stern and solid, with the wrought-iron gates which would look well on any presbytery wall.

Padre Capello

All those who have studied in Rome knew Father Capello, the famous canonist, who died not so very long ago. A frail, transparent little man who knew the Code of Canon Law by heart, Fr Capello was one of Rome's most famous confessors. He heard confessions early in the morning and yet always had a queue. Even in his lifetime he enjoyed the reputation of a saint. His grave lies inside the Jesuit mausoleum, just to the left inside the wrought-iron gates.

At this week-end, crowds knelt all day outside the gates. The superintendent told me that there were five informal processions in Fr Capello's honour yesterday. Today there were banks of flowers round the gates.

Seeing such enthusiasm, one begins to grasp the problems which face Northern people when they hope that one of their townsfolk will be canonized. Archbishop Chichester lies beyond Fr Capello in the vault. He died during the Council and certainly is not forgotten either in England or Rhodesia. Yet I for one had never thought of bringing flowers and he, an Englishman in heaven, would have been mightily embarrassed if I had.

Outside my door

Across the road from where I live stands a famous hospital in which St Camillus de Lellis is said to have worked. On my side of the road, facing the hospital entrance, a cunning undertaker has fixed up an advert which fits against the kerb. The bereaved, their eyes sorrowful and downcast, read the notice as they cross the road. Could you imagine St George's Hospital, London, allowing an advertisement for funerals on the pavement outside the emergency door? Which only goes to show how different is the outlook of different nations and how clever the Church must be to cater for the idiosyncrasies of all.

Tailpiece

An American priest told me yesterday of an amusing conversation which he had, last week, with a South American. Said the South American, "I cannot understand how the United States, so large and progressive a democracy, is so far behind in counting its votes. Why, you have a congressional election and it takes you a week or more to know the full results. In my country, we know the results six weeks before the election is due to start."

ITALIAN QUARTET

No. 1

"Now you have seen the whole house," she said, smiling at me, "except that I have not shown you my daughter's rooms."

"Is she at home?" I asked.

"No, she left last week for a shooting party near Milan. She needed a bit of a change, poor dear, after a heavy cold."

So I saw Augusta's rooms and was duly surprised. It is not so easy to count while carrying on a polite conversation, but there must have been thirty bottles of beauty lotions on the dressing-table, ten pairs of scissors, not to mention tubes, brushes, pads.

The dressing-table was, however, only a passing distraction: the eye was held by a fantastic display of animals in all kinds of materials. I counted fifty-three without looking round. They were of china, porcelain, glass, wool, straw, metal, plastic, staring down at me from mantelpiece, walls, cupboards, through their beady, MacFishery eyes.

A basket-work scorpion climbed the mirror, two glass reindeer grazed peacefully on the bed-table, three green china frogs were gargling on the top of the bookcase, while a bullfight with sixteen pieces was in full cry on the shelf beneath.

High on the wall and all askew hung a sad Madonna with animals dangling on threads from her frame.

"Some dusting," said I.

"Oh," she said, "the servants do that!"

"How old is Augusta?" I asked.

"Let me see; in May she will be nineteen."

We returned to the drawing-room.

"I don't know," she remarked sadly; "Augusta is very difficult. It is not as though I had not given her absolutely everything, and my husband too." She thought a while and added, pouting, "I'm pretty sure that she has lost her faith."

"Why would that be?" asked I.

She was quick with her answer, "Well, frankly," she remarked, "I blame the nuns; they spoilt her at school!"

No. 2

Yes, you still meet old fascists in Italy, quiet, respectable, elderly people of all classes, who admit the errors, think savagely of Hitler but remember Benito Mussolini with deep affection, even love.

I was shown his signed photograph; the Duce, proud and magnificent on horseback in those early golden days. There was a copper bust of him with his name engraved across the base. "No," they said, "even in the time of his disgrace when everyone turned against him, we never put this away!"

For Mussolini in his prime and in the privacy of friendship was, without doubt, an amusing and lovable man. "At least he gave us enthusiasm," they said, "and a great love for our country; qualities not in good supply today."

As I turned the old albums and saw once again the photographs of Ciano, Grandi, Badoglio, Balbo and Prince Umberto, someone asked me, shyly, if I would like to hear the Duce's voice?

Of course I would. I had seen him on his balcony when I was a boy. Strange to be gazing out over Eternal Rome and listening to the canned applause and laughter

76

from the great crowd in the Piazza Venetia twenty-five years ago. Oh, for a record of Mark Antony's voice with a background of forum noises, or of Henry VIII's to reveal for good what kind of a man he was. How thrilling history lessons will be in the not too distant future when one will no more have to judge a man only from books.

Mussolini's crowds laughed and cheered so much that he himself did not need to say very much. He sounded cold and restrained by modern television standards and spoke so slowly that even I could follow every word. There was in his voice a paternal note of deep affection and one noted the skill with which he could make the crowd stand absolutely silent and then, as swiftly, laugh. The twenty-five years since he made that particular speech had turned his voice more mellow and made both his claims and himself seem very small.

Of the two teenagers who were listening with me, one, with a shrug, remarked, "The same old rubbish." The other did not speak but his eyes were bright.

The Italians do things nicely. They have not forgotten Mussolini, they are both grateful and forgiving, though they would not want him back. The modern fascist party is up to date and different; the old guard, now respectable, sober and rheumatic, are not prepared to deny the pleasure and excitement which he gave them in his first, triumphant days.

The monument to Clara Pettaci, Benito's mistress, stands in the cemetery of San Lorenzo and was banked with flowers on All Hallows E'en. As one Italian put it to me, with that simple sense of reality which is always so attractive, "At least, unlike most of us, she was very brave!"

77

Federico hails from Milan. On his mother's side his family goes back to Romulus and Remus with hardly a break. His father had an ancestor who fought the Moors in Spain and another who fought the Turks at Lepanto while his brother was buying real estate in Tuscany. Federico's coat-of-arms is colourful but, as he has recently discovered, a coat-of-arms by itself will not keep out the cold.

Federico looks aristocratic and obeys the laws laid down by pundits, his wrists are slender and his ankles thin. He is, in fact, very like a whippet and shares that high-class animal's superior grace. He is elegant in his studio, even in his shirt sleeves, and would like to be able to look Bohemian. He is doomed for ever to look as though he were commanding at Lepanto though he does not feel aristocratic and hates ships.

Federico, as a little boy, lived under the German occupation, using to the sentries, when he was barely seven, words which older men avoid for the sake of their skins. Later, rather than live for ever on the credit of Romulus and Remus, he joined an air line as an interpreter. The effort bored him and he left.

His life changed with two novel acquisitions, a small German camera and a lovely, New England wife. Never before had so close a descendant of Romulus and Remus linked up with Boston, Mass. Nor did his family care very much for his little camera, his amateur excursions to photograph factory equipment, his midnight labours as he developed his plates in the kitchen sink.

Federico is self-taught. Now one of the best-known photographers in the North, he specializes on selling American soap.

Federico works impossibly long hours and deserves every penny that he earns. It is a thrill to watch him in his superb studio, photographing a professional mother and a still more professional baby to help to sell an American 'two-way' soap. If we are to believe the jargon, this soap penetrates the pores of the skin with a double cleansing action and never comes out by the way it went in!

Federico excites the baby, stimulates it, flashes lights in its eyes, pays men to wave to distract its attention, shouts like a matador citing a bull. Thirty-two plates were needed before he could capture that expression of love, hygiene, deodorized maternal rapture which, in its turn, will capture the suckers back home. Federico does not sell soap himself—he is descended from Romulus and Remus—but he uses his genius to get a mother and baby, who met in his studio that morning, so to love each other before his camera that the soft soap is bound to sell.

His wife and children keep him human, for I doubt if the task of making money out of suckers, who will get it back out of other suckers, will ever fully satisfy his artistic sense. He is an aristocrat who has beaten the Smart Alecks at their own game. A man of thought, however, cannot easily stop thinking about the emptiness of modern life.

The General Council means nothing to Federico, for his life is full of American 'two-way' soap. His family has been Christian since the days of Constantine. There are saints in the family, too, a brace of Cardinals in the Middle Ages, and all those warriors who died to defeat the Turks. Federico certainly calls himself a Catholic and he loves antiques. His children will inherit his wealth and his camera but not much faith. He is as 'two-way' as the soap he is plugging; he will not come out the way he went in.

No. 4

I will never forget Hazel's outburst, for it struck a sad and discordant note. Up to that time we had had a most informal and friendly evening in a small, top-floor flat. A journalist and his wife were hosts. We had with us an American missionary and a young Commonwealth monsignor. I cannot recall his country, but he was an understudy in the Roman Curia. There was also Hazel, a smart and pretty girl from California, who had studied art and drama and was polishing up her Italian in Rome. Hazel was not a Catholic, the rest of us were.

Food had been ferried from the kitchen; we had all wandered about, pretending to help others but mainly helping ourselves. There was Frascati wine in plenty and I wondered, later, if Hazel had not had too much.

She looked very sober and very normal and her out-burst was unexpected and embarrassing.

We were talking about the Council and this itself annoyed her, though she listened thoughtfully. She pointed out that she was not a Catholic, that she did not mind hearing about the Council, but that it was getting pretty dull after two months. So we changed the subject, chatted about California for a few moments and then gradually began moving back to Rome. The Commonwealth monsignor, being a curial official, was fair game for the journalists!

Someone praised Rome and I, who loved the city and its people, hastened to agree. As I spoke in its praise, I could see Hazel staring at me with her lips quivering and anger in her eyes. This was rather disconcerting, but I thought it better to continue, guessing that soon she would intervene. She gave no indication and I had no way of knowing the cause of her distress. Was she just anti-Catholic and was the clerical atmosphere and the talk about the Council getting on her nerves? We were soon to know. Speaking very slowly, Hazel inter-rupted to put a question: "Father," she said, and she was very much in earnest, "do you really like Rome? Do you really mean what you say?"

"Why, yes, of course," I answered. "Don't you?"

"It is a filthy place," she said vehemently, "and I am astonished that you priests can so fool yourselves."

"Whatever is the matter, Hazel?" I asked, puzzled.

"Father"—she almost shouted the word—"the Roman men are filthy and you sit there preening your-selves. A girl cannot go on a bus, cannot walk in the street without being handled and pinched. If they only stared at you it would be bad enough, and I would think them filthy, but what is the use of a city full of shrines

81

and Madonnas when men lack the control to keep their hands to themselves. We girls have to think twice before we walk down some of the streets. I come from California, I am not a Catholic, nor am I used to such a blatant public attack on a girl's modesty."

The Commonwealth monsignor looked on the floor, the American missionary felt moved to say something, but it was my friend the journalist who got there first.

"I would not know about these things, Hazel," he said kindly, "but surely you can call the police."

Hazel exploded. "The police!" she said, frantically, and then went on to flay the police force, all of whom had been so very courteous to me. "What is more," she cried, almost in tears, "the worst place in Rome is the Piazza of St Peter's and you know nothing and do nothing about these things."

Hazel left the room crying and I have not seen her since. We others made excuses for her, pointing out that she was young, that California is different, that she was hysterical, that she might have drunk too much.

I think that we might have condemned Hazel for her outburst, had not the only other woman in the party checked us with two simple words, "It's true."

I have since asked several other sensible women of all ages, and five out of six support Hazel's point of view. You and I know very well the immodesties of London and we are not prudes. I am a man and I would not know one way or the other and, Hazel or no Hazel, I love Rome very much.

For myself, I would have omitted Hazel's story in such a friendly and happy book. But Hazel herself was annoyed that a priest should be so naïve on a vital subject and some readers, possibly non-Catholic, might know what Hazel knows. If Hazel is right, and I will never see her again to tell her, I would like to have given a non-Catholic Californian's view of Roman life. I cannot support it or deny it and I love Rome just the same. But if Hazel is right, the Romans should do something about it, because the Council, the shrines, the Madonnas look both tawdry and tragic if decent women are afraid to walk in the Roman streets.

Said I to a friend who had read the manuscript, "Should I omit the story of Hazel?" After two days he replied, "I have spoken to my wife, who knows Rome well; publish it."

NUNS IN AN AUSTIN VAN

OFFICIALLY, nuns had no place in the Vatican Council;
they were not consulted about the founts of revelation
and, if they had been, would have made no reply. Behind the scenes, however, the sisters laboured without
ceasing, and both the Council and its Fathers owed
much to their devoted care. They nursed, sewed, cooked,
scrubbed, and even ran the Post Office just inside the
Vatican arcade. On the very day before the opening of
the Vatican Council, while journalists and monsignori
hurried past with bulging briefcases, three little nuns,
entirely unruffled, sat on the altar steps of St Peter's
sewing the carpet that led to the papal throne.

The sisters looked sweet and innocent, but all who
knew Rome intimately warned us that they were not
so green. Full habits and long sleeves gave them a frailty
and asceticism which concealed their inner strength.
Besides, nuns all push or pull together and thus achieve
the force of a tug-o'-war team.

In the surging crowds in St Peter's and its piazza, the

sisters rode like corks. Some said that they carried knives, but I saw no evidence of that. Whenever I saw a nun she was demure and modest, and one never bothered to enquire how she managed to reach the front seat. Could it be that the Swiss Guards, the Palatine Guards, the Noble Guards, the gendarmes and monsignori all have sisters or aunts in convents and know that it is wiser to give way gracefully? Seminarians are caught, middle-aged priests like myself are rounded up, cordoned off and lassoed in hundreds, but I never saw a nun who was stopped from doing as she pleased. His Holiness was scarcely out of his basilica on the Sedia Gestatoria when the nuns took over the church. As the bishops left, the nuns moved in. I saw them sitting in the bishops' seats, testing the voting system; on their knees in the gangways examining the underneath of the conciliar stalls. "I told you, Mother, they are just held with drawing pins," drawled an Australian nun to her Reverend Mother, seated on a cardinal's throne above.

Out in the piazza, the sisters also held sway. Gendarmes were there, burly priests, pilgrims who had come a long way to see very little, but the sisters again had pride of place. Was there a Reverend Mother with a walkie-talkie, hidden inside the colonnade? The sisters never raised their eyes, they spoke in whispers and looked as meek as St Gemma Galgani, but got there just the same.

As the prelates came out of St Peter's after each morning session, the nuns were there to greet them and even to take their photographs. Language barriers and crowd barriers prove no problem to nuns. Archbishops and archimandrites smiled benignly as a Little Sister of the Holy Sepulchre stepped forward with her Zeiss. The phrase of the *Magnificat* which once so deeply troubled King Roger of Sicily was also verified today.

But in 1962 we faced a further challenge from the nuns on wheels. Few bishops will forget the traffic jams on the roads outside St Peter's as forty-six buses packed with prelates debauched into the Roman streets. Pigeons circled, the faithful cheered, the journalists hunted around for gossip, the tourists waved their handkerchiefs and begged for blessings while the nuns packed themselves into their little cars. Eight full-grown nuns in an Austin van was the then record, but by now this will have been many times excelled.

I met this Austin van. Usually I went home on foot, but a Conciliar theologian had offered me a lift when the session was over and I climbed in outside the studio of Vatican Radio.

Ours was a big car, hired by a Texan prelate, but it cut small ice with the Roman police. We had to wait, prelate and all, the bishops in buses were held at the barrier while the eight Little Sisters of the Holy Sepulchre drove out in their Austin van. They were demure and sombre, probably examining their consciences. There was no sign of exultation on their Italian faces as they left all of us, cardinals, bishops, Texan theogians, behind.

I forget the name of the street, but we overtook them at the turning by the Columbus hotel. The sisters all turned their heads to the left and dipped their eyes in unison before our purple, but Reverend Mother, sitting next to the sister driver, gazed straight ahead. No doubt she had never heard of Z Cars, but she looked the part.

Once we had passed, I could see through the driving mirror that the Little Sisters had no intention of being left in second place. Examination of conscience over for the moment, they were leaning forward to egg Sister

Chauffeur on. Their horn had a peremptory note about it, though the arrangement of its tootles fitted the midday Angelus. The sisters turned their heads to the right and dropped their eyes in respect as they passed us, Reverend Mother looking straight ahead.

In the Via Dei Penitenzieri, with bus loads of bishops before and behind us, our race with the Little Sisters of the Holy Sepulchre really got under way. We passed them outside the hospital, they caught us by the tunnel, we turning sharply on two wheels, they sharper on no wheels at all. The Little Sisters of the Holy Sepulchre turned their heads to right or left in unison, dipping their eyes in reverence even when they overtook us on the wrong side. Reverend Mother stared, fixedly, ahead.

The policeman at the junction, poised aloft in his precarious pulpit, raised his arm to check our flight. Our Texan driver slowed down just as he would have done in Dallas unless he wanted a bullet through his chest. The Little Sisters of the Holy Sepulchre also slowed for a moment and, out of modesty, while our cars were level, dipped their eyes while looking straight ahead.

I think that the Sister Chauffeur meant to stop, but Reverend Mother said something to her and, in a spirit of complete and blind obedience, she zoomed ahead. My American friend, who knew Italian, swore that he heard the words "Step on it, Sister!" as they drew across the line of traffic, swerved right and left to miss the policeman and vanished out of sight.

The policeman blew his whistle, abandoned his pulpit and the traffic and stalked majestically to our Texan car. In a few choice phrases and with invocations to Our Lady, St Joseph, Fanfani and Toggliati, he told us, as far as I could gather, what he would like to do with our necks.

"Say," said my Texan friend with dignity, "what about those sisters?"

"Where would we be without them?" said the policeman piously, grinning like the Neapolitan he was.

THE TEST MATCH

CRICKET may need reforming, but this is no concern of the Church. Yet there are cricketers in the General Council, an English bishop who once kept wicket for the English College, an Indian who was a promising bowler, two Australians who were members of the Melbourne Cricket Club. One was also told of five ecumenically-minded Germans who are preparing a scientific study of the game which our separated brethren so much love.

On the second day of the Test Match at Brisbane, there was small excitement as the bishops drove up in buses to start the morning's work. Spanish bishops paced in pairs discussing, not cricket, but Salamanca and a possible case of heresy found near there.

The French and the German bishops took the steps slowly, not because they were worried about the Brisbane wicket but because they were carrying the pastoral burdens of the Church. One Australian bishop is said to have bowled an imaginary 'chinaman' to a non-existent Dexter, to the horror of a nearby archimandrite who already entertained jaundiced views of the Western Church.

No, the Test Match counted for nothing, and yet it may be asserted without fear of contradiction that the feats of Booth, Mackay and Trueman were known and pondered deep in the heart of Rome.

It all began with an Irish priest whose father had won the O.B.E. in the 1916 troubles and had been a cricketer of some repute. Son followed father and, on this occasion, popped out between Lauds and breakfast to reach Vatican Radio, where a friend had promised him the scores. He was told, or so he swears, that at close of play England were 120 for two. Dexter had scored twenty-two runs off Richie Benaud in fourteen balls.

The son of the Irish O.B.E. slipped back to the community breakfast without a stir. He passed the news to a neighbouring Dutchman just as this good man had raised a bowl of steaming coffee to his lips. The Dutchman lowered the coffee, not permitting himself even a teeny sip. He must phone his bosom friend, a Lateran professor, for whom cricket was the only link with normal life.

This Lateran professor started work at 4 a.m., except on Tuesdays or in Paschal-tide. He lowered the Dead Sea scrolls which he was delousing as soon as the telephone rang. He himself played no cricket, but he knew Wisden by heart. His father had once, in the good old days, captained 'the Gentlemen of Rotterdam'. He now said, "Ach Dexter, Dexter, Dexter!" several times. He then phoned the College of Propaganda to inform Monsignor Pondicherry that Dexter had made 120 off twenty-two balls.

Indians and Pakistanis alike take a perennial interest in cricket, especially when Australia plays England and one of the two is bound to lose. The Indians and Pakistanis are tired of losing themselves. Propaganda phoned the Norland Hotel and the Minerva, and the Indian bishops arrived at the Council with Dexter at 200 not out.

Had the son of the Irish O.B.E. been our only informant, Dexter might have broken all records by now. Alas, there was another fount of revelation, for Fr Daly of Adelaide, theological adviser for the *schema* on the means of mass communication, rose at 5.30 a.m. to get Brisbane on his radio, direct. He heard with horror that England were 120 for two and that Dexter had scored twenty-two off Richie Benaud in fourteen balls. Being Australian, he refused to leave the set until his faith in Richie Benaud had been restored. He therefore listened to the last few overs and knew that Dexter had been caught.

With Dexter out, Fr Daly phoned the Bishop of Pepsi-Cola (Queensland, not Nebraska) and the bishop was not annoyed to be roused at such an hour for such glorious news. With no spare paper in his bedroom, he jotted down the scores on the top of the address which he was to deliver in the Council chamber that very day. He hoped to have some fun in the coffee bar later, chipping the English hierarchy.

When His Excellency started his address to the Council in fluent Latin, the word Dexter, written in pencil, shot off his tongue. German, Spanish and French bishops nodded wisely, for this was a Latin word which they all knew. The Australian bishop was, thus, saved by Dexter; with a certain amount of coughing to cover his embarrassment, he got back to the text. But for Dexter he might have had the unusual record of being the very first bishop in any General Council since Nicaea who had announced the cricket scores.

In the coffee bar later there was a good deal of chaffing, but the fact was clear that Dexter was out. The English bishops were unbelieving; they had had it from the College of Propaganda itself that he had made over a hundred off twenty-two balls. They admitted that the figures sounded very fishy but, after all, the Australian bowling was pretty weak. Anyhow, the General Council was the General Council, so both the Australian and British bishops turned back to the hall and to the things that really count.

One bishop did not turn back. His Excellency the Bishop of the Diamond Isles had been born in Clapham and, as a boy, had visited the Oval on every free and sunny day. He had been out of England for forty years and had not bothered about cricket since the summer of 1923. Now, of a sudden, this unexpected conversation about Dexter had brought back to him all the excitement of former days. Yes, the Bishop of the Diamond Isles was excited and also slightly ashamed of himself. Yet he knew himself too well, knew that he could never settle down again to the matter of Christian Reunion until he knew for certain of Dexter's fate.

The little old missionary bishop slipped out and phoned the College of Propaganda on the sly. He felt young and wicked again. When the voice at the other end said, "Pronto, Pronto, Pronto," he put his question, "Was Dexter really out?" The voice at the other end thought that he was asking for the Rector, who was certainly out for dinner; the bishop had to shout Dexter many times. It took a full five minutes before an Australian voice came over the phone to assure him that Dexter was undoubtedly out.

"What about Hobbs?" The Bishop of the Diamond Isles knew before he asked that he was silly, that there could never be an answer, that Jack Hobbs was now no better remembered than the Barberini Pope. Still, he just had to ask the question as he had so often done in Clapham forty years ago.

"You could do with Hobbs," remarked the Australian voice, kindly, and the Bishop of the Diamond Isles was glad.

THE BISHOPS PACK THEIR MITRES

So it is all over. The bishops pack their mitres and depart. The pavement theologians face a bleak future. They will probably eat each other now that their daily ration of gossip has been stopped at the source.

The Pope

The most lasting and moving memory of the General Council has been the humility of His Holiness the Pope. Eyes turn automatically to the top floor, right, of the Vatican Palace, to two rooms which have their lights on half the night. There lives the most loved, most loving, most lonely man in the world. The illness of the Pope has given rise to a host of rumours that have saddened the session's dying days. Yet the spirit of the Pope has so stamped its courage upon all and sundry that everyone looks fearlessly ahead. If His Holiness is not there for the next session, his work will certainly go forward with determination; somehow everyone is secretly certain that he will be there.

The Bishops

The daily sight of the bishops, treading and threading their way to and from St Peter's has brought home vividly the holiness and Catholicity of the Church. Catholicity may be studied in the Council photographs, but Kodak cannot snap holiness.

You need to have lived in Rome, with a working knowledge of episcopal shortcomings in previous centuries, to grasp how good our modern bishops are.

Many have been up as early as 5 a.m. to offer Mass in relays before leaving for St Peter's at 8 o'clock.

They walk the streets humbly, talk to everyone, greet everyone, support every kind of apostolic undertaking, and are probably in bed with a cup of Ovaltine at half-past ten. Their conversation is shrewd and highly amusing, their eyes are on the Council programme, but their hearts have been at home. For many of us the bishops of the Church now look like fathers where, before the Council, they were as rare and as aloof as admirals of the fleet.

The Jesters

Medieval kings paid jesters to keep the nation happy by publicly pulling their legs. Democracies need no jesters—they are, too often, a bit of a joke themselves. Rome as a monarchy is rich in jests. They even point out for you the small room on the second floor of the Holy Office in which a batch of monsignori of all nationalities work out the daily jokes.

In place of the traditional Englishman, Irishman and Scotsman, we, here, have had Cardinals X, Y, and Z. The daily doings of these admirable prelates lead all who have a sense of humour to love the Church. Some of the best of the jokes have come from the bishops themselves. So when the Irish and South African hierarchies were invited to the conference of Commonwealth bishops, one of them replied with a wink, "I think we had better send observers!"

A change of mind

Optimists and pessimists alike agree that a new spirit has been released in this session which cannot be confined. The optimists are sure that the next session, starting in the summer, will be the more successful because of the many lessons acquired in the first. One most striking feature of the discussions now ending has been an astonishing openness of mind. Thus an Australian bishop, in a radio address from the Vatican studios to his country, openly admitted that he had left for the Council with his mind made up on many points. He had taken advice on important matters and thought that he knew the truth. After the Conciliar debates and when he had heard the point of view of other bishops from different countries and with different problems, he had been forced to change his mind. How few people in middle age, how few members of parliament, ever change their minds! It is for most of us a whole time and hazardous exercise to accept a new idea, to break a habit, to admit a mistake.

The final Mass

In a city as conservative as Rome, the General Council session ended with a great sensation for the *Missa De Angelis* took the place of the normal polyphony of Palestrina and Bartolucci on Saturday for the closing Mass.

After an official announcement had provided the details of the polyphonic music to be sung by the Sistine choir, the Council Fathers expressed the urgent desire to sing the Mass themselves. The Secretary General, Mgr Felici, announced this request in the Council hall on Friday, and the applause which followed made clear the Council's mind.

In place of the Sistine choir, the Gregorian choir from San Anselmo stood near to the vested statue of St Peter on the Epistle side of the nave. A Benedictine monk mounted the Council rostrum to conduct the bishops in the *Missa De Angelis*.

Surprise and enthusiasm showed immediately in every part of the crowded basilica, and many who had been attending pontifical functions for years not only rubbed their eyes but raised their voices in delight. The choral singing was excellent, and a Mass which would normally have taken at least two hours was finished with exquisite grace and dignity in one.

This sudden change of mind in Rome may be attributed to many causes, of which the first was the dissatisfaction expressed after the glorious opening Mass. On that great occasion, with all the bishops of the world present, the vast congregation hardly sang one note.

The mind of the bishops changed with the daily experience of community Mass during the Council, with all the bishops participating in the responses spontaneously. Many bishops in radio talks during, and about, the Council expressed their personal delight and pleasure at this community exercise. Mass was celebrated in many different rites, was offered facing the congregation, was, as it should be, the unifying act of the Council as a whole. The liturgy which the Conciliar Fathers discussed for a month they also lived themselves.

What is the mind of the Pope? Last year, at a huge pilgrimage from France, the congregation took over the singing of the Creed from the official choir without being asked. The spontaneous joy of all and the magnificent singing greatly moved the Pope. In his address to the pilgrims, His Holiness went out of his way to praise the undoubted excellence of the Sistine choir, but remarked, with feeling, how much he loved to hear the

Creed sung as it had been sung by the pilgrims that day.

So the final Mass of the session was sung in unison by the Council Fathers, and this is regarded by all who know Rome and its traditions as a very significant liturgical change. Unfortunately it can only happen when there is a body of bishops or pilgrims to sing. The normal Roman congregation is not yet prepared to sing a note.

Traditions die slowly. Today, the Council over, St Peter's is again jammed to the doors for a canonization ceremony. The Sistine choir is back with its polyphony, beautifully performed. Yet for all the skill, today's Mass lacks the participation of the people and the enthusiasm which was so marked, so much appreciated, yesterday. The Creed has just been sung by some six voices, though thousands upon thousands pack the church. It is still too soon to speculate, but it looks as though today's ceremony will take three hours and a half.

THE CANONIZATIONS

I END my stay in Rome where I began, in the balcony high above St Peter's tomb. The commentators are here; we crouch before our microphones, exchanging places without a sound. His Holiness the Pope is seated on a throne in the far distance at the end of the apse. He looked tired and frail when he entered the basilica, but his powers of recovery are extraordinary; he has just spoken in a firm voice for half an hour, first in Latin, then in Italian, then in French.

These canonization ceremonies are far more gay and more Italian than the Council sessions and ceremonies. At 7.30 a.m., when I reached the piazza of St Peter's, it was jammed with buses bringing pilgrims from all over Italy to honour the two new Italian saints. The pilgrims had an unexpected thrill, for the fountains had wet the ground, which had then frozen, leaving us to negotiate most dangerous patches of ice. I saw pilgrims on the ground, pilgrims picking themselves up, young pilgrims pushing each other, slipping, falling to the ground. All were laughing, even the girl who had fallen and hurt her nose.

Thoughtful mothers were stuffing the pockets of young seminarians with biscuits, fruit and bottles of Coke. There were hundreds of lads dressed in Franciscan habits and swanking, unless they were trying to beat each other with their cords. Seminarians, too, ran by in cottas, shouting and laughing. Some of them looked frighteningly young.

As I arrived, a miniature cavalry charge was launched. Away they all ran, up the steps and into St Peter's and down the side-aisle at a trot.

Inside St Peter's one was immediately reminded of the Mansion House Station at 6.30 p.m. The young seminarians, in fine fettle, had reached a crash barrier designed to check enthusiasm such as theirs. While they heaved and pushed to get through first, five perspiring Capuchins were passing trays of vestments over their heads. I found myself pinned against a confessional whose sharp corner was playing havoc with my spine.

Eventually the seminarians made the nave. At the word of an official, they swooped with joy on the stalls of the Council Fathers, now for the first time unoccupied. Naturally enough there was a tussle to have the Cardinals' pews. Three bearded bishops, sitting together at the back discussing theology, were certainly startled when the younger generation swarmed on every side.

Sadly enough, the official had been wrong. An even higher official arrived, out of breath and in a fluster, and the poor young seminarians were rounded up. They were despatched to a gallery above, where they sat seeing practically nothing for three hours and a half. On the way out, after the ceremony, they looked far more sombre and recollected; poor things, their long, long training had begun!

Let no reader be so foolish as to think that the cavalry charge and other excitements described were irreverent even in this Mother Church. The great crowd, happy and friendly, was as reverent as you and I might be at home. It was this homeliness which touched me most.

A kind American seminarian—one could recognize

his slouch from a great distance—told me of the wager which he had had with some colleagues that he would get into the basilica without a ticket for this canonization day. Twice he had nearly succeeded by walking in with a group of bishops, but eventually he had been caught. The third time he was successful for, thoughtfully, he had brought a small suitcase with him and this he officially surrendered to a man collecting such objects at one of the doors. He was given a cloakroom ticket and this carried weight with the many guards.

He has promised to show me a quick way out of St Peter's, so I must dash off to find him now.

THE CATACOMB LAMPS

AT the close of the first session of the General Council, many found it difficult to pack. Bishops could scarcely find room for the many souvenirs which they had collected, and yet these are usually too sacred or too bulky to be thrown away. Pious objects are virtually indestructible. Those with sufficient cunning fob them off on others and, for this very reason, wise old residents make the resolution never to speak in private to those who are departing the next day.

I was an innocent. After tearful adieus to secretaries, theologians, bishops, I could hardly stagger home with my pious souvenirs. I had a copper medal of an Avignon Pope, a portrait of Pope Pius X done in seashells, sixteen glass slides of Conciliar Fathers and fourteen green, bronze catacomb lamps. The latter are exceptionally heavy and of very little use. No doubt the originals were valuable in time of persecution; fourteen imitations are less precious in these enlightened days.

When my turn came to leave the Eternal City, few innocents were left to accept them and the bottom of the Tiber seemed their most likely resting place. Easier said than done. Even in Rome one would have looked slightly conspicuous hanging over the embankment to drop fourteen green, bronze catacombe lamps into the stream below. Rather than carry them with me, I think I would have risked the river had not a colleague mentioned a convent further down the road.

He drew for me a touching picture of the bright-eyed

Roman orphans aching to take a green, bronze catacomb lamp to bed. Wiping away a tear and inwardly exulting, I made a hurried note of the address.

Reverend Mother sailed into the parlour to greet me with a stern Sister Commissar by her side. There were the usual diplomatic bows, a few words from me about the heroism of their labours and a few kind words about England and its conversion by Reverend Mother in reply. Both sides bowed low again and the faint sound of scraping metal gave the show away. Reverend Mother, hearing the sound, became more chilly, while I was tempted to dump the lamps in the parlour and run away.

Roman diplomacy would not tolerate such an exhibition and Reverend Mother, smiling, heard me out. She nodded slightly as the seashell portrait of the saintly pontiff was first mentioned and then displayed. If she did not formulate her refusal in words, her manner became so full of Christian perfection that it became clear that she did not want to see another green, bronze catacomb lamp for the rest of her life. Indeed, she had even started an involved sentence which would have ended in a flat refusal when the Sister Commissar beside her cleared her throat.

I do not know the conventual form for kicking a person under the table but, whatever it was, the Sister Commissar had done it to some effect. Reverend Mother ended her opening sentence on a preposition, a thing that Reverend Mothers rarely do. Further, she bowed and smiled and then went back to start again.

She said that priests were always so thoughtful about her orphans, that English priests were exceptionally kind-hearted and that Jesuits were outstanding in their care for God's little ones. I gathered that the said little ones were panting for the portrait of Pope Pius X in sea-shells and that the green, bronze catacomb lamps would be kept until Christmas, when there would be jubilee indeed!

Even Sister Commissar smiled in approval, and the plastic bag containing all these treasures was solemnly transferred. I begged Reverend Mother not to mention it and, if she wanted, to keep the plastic bag.

We were near to the front door—a cup of tea offered but not accepted—when Reverend Mother paused with her most winning smile. I had shown myself so kind to the orphans that she was sure that I would also do a small favour to the community.

Wiser priests would, at this moment, have bolted and not looked back till they reached the Pincio. I was stupid. Besides, Sister Commissar had slipped away un-noticed and now stood with her back to the main door.

Taking my consent for granted, Reverend Mother asked, as I was leaving Rome tomorrow, would I take two small parcels to the sisters in London as a Christmas present from the community in Rome? Blanching, I nodded assent. Reverend Mother said that the parcels would be quite small and handy, that the English Customs men were so understanding, that the parcels would be at my house early on the following day.

I could not now swear to it but I rather think that Sister Commissar winked.

At Dover, the Customs men eyed the two wooden crates with some suspicion and asked me what they contained. "I have not a clue," said I, "but my guess would be at least fourteen green, bronze catacomb lamps."

"Well, let's see, shall we?" said the officials pleasantly, calling a nearby cooper to open up the crates.

Yes, there was the Avignon Pope in copper, Pope Pius X in seashells, and the green, bronze catacomb lamps. Along with them was a goodly amount of other rubbish, broken rosaries, holy pictures and thousands of second-hand Christmas cards.

"Better open up all the boxes, Joe," said one fellow to another. "With nuns you never know!" Dover had never seen such confusion since it was hit in the war.

"Nothing dutiable," said the Customs men, after wishing me a very happy Christmas, "but we would love to know what is the exact purpose of these green, bronze lamps?"

It is part of the sturdy British sense of justice that I had to pay ten shillings to the cooper; he, like the Roman orphans, has to live.

EPILOGUE

OUTCASTS OF INDIA

APPEALS by missionaries are so plentiful and money so hard to come by that one is forced to drop most of them into the paper basket while looking the other way.

For me the appeal from Fr Alfred Nevett seemed different. First, the very name *Outcast* or *Pariah* speaks of poverty and dejection in its lowest and most horrifying form. Next, the outcasts about whom he wrote were Catholics from that very part of India which St Francis Xavier visited first. They are the descendants of those pearl fishers whom the saint loved so much. Finally, Fr Nevett himself is an Englishman whom I had known thirty-five years ago. Nor was he asking for clothes or money as a palliative but was proposing a simple scheme whereby the depressed peoples of Southern India could be lifted out of themselves.

The Scheme

Fr Nevett's contention is this: that the outcasts of Madurai will remain in squalor and depression until the children are trained for better jobs. He asserts that the Indian Government has made a serious effort to assist them but, so extreme is the poverty of these good Catholic people, that it will take decades to improve their lot.

On the other hand, immediate results could be obtained if Christian people started on a small scale to establish groups of scholarships. Individual children could be sent away at once for schooling while waiting for the larger and more complicated national schemes to start.

Before I left for Rome in September, I inserted a small paragraph in the *Catholic Herald* saying no more than is written above. £40 came in in the first week. One cheque was sent by a Lancashire business man. He gave us £25 in painful circumstances. After years of longing, his wife was expecting her first child. He had promised £25 to the Indian Outcasts if his prayers were answered and the baby was safely born. This was not to be. The child had died but he did not see why the poor Indians should be the poorer for his own cruel loss.

We forwarded the £40 to Fr Nevett, whose answer was a very great pleasure and surprise. £40 would send three children to school for a year, and so Louis, Frederick and Mary had been despatched. Fr Nevett sent 'thank you' notes from the three children to the benefactors over here. He also sent detailed replies to questions which we had asked him, and while these make grim reading they also hold out hope. I publish them in full.

Q. *Please give us a picture of the situation with which you are trying to cope.*

A. Imagine a large pond of stagnant water, situated some five feet below the level of the mud road. The water stinks from afar off since it is mostly sewage and is also used as a public latrine—a common practice in slum areas since the slum houses have no conveniences and public latrines are few and far between. Below the road and on the edge of this stagnant water are over a hundred houses, crowded together and touching each other. Each house is 10 ft by 4 ft, made of palm trees;

roof, walls and all. A leafy bower may sound fine in a poem, but it is of no use at all in a slum. The leaves do not keep out the heavy rain; they soon rot, leaving many holes. Sometimes goats and water buffaloes, which wander where they please, make holes in the sides of the houses or knock them down.

Since the roof leaks and the water off the road runs down into the houses, these are always damp in the rainy season. People in these houses are always sick and, due to overcrowding, lack of sanitation and hygiene, diseases soon spread around. Dysentery and typhoid seem to be endemic.

In a house of this kind lives a young Catholic couple with their four children, Mary, Maggee, a little two-year-old sister and a baby brother. They also give shelter to a grown-up cousin.

Inside the house, in one corner, is the kitchen, two stones and a cooking vessel; on the wall opposite are pictures of the Sacred Heart, Our Lady and St Antony, a very popular saint in these parts.

In the house would be two tin boxes to hold clothes and everything else. One or two old tins suffice for all the possessions of the family. In fact with seven people in the house already, there is no room for anything else. The father is a coolie, but since he is an asthma case he finds it very difficult to keep a job.

Another family lives in a similar house. Here the father is a cripple. He was knocked down by a lorry and his leg so badly smashed that now it is only a useless, dry stick. In a country where healthy young men find it difficult to get a job, he stands no chance of employment. There are two boys and two girls, the youngest being two years old. Since the father is a cripple and cannot chase after the toddlers, one of the

107

elder girls is held back from school to mind them. The family is supported by the mother, who works carrying bricks on building jobs and does the house chores early in the morning or late at night.

This will give you some idea of the general conditions in the slums, the dwelling places of most of our Harijan Catholics.

Q. *Which children would you pick for Scholarships?*
A. In the beginning I would pick children known to me personally. I have in mind some very poor families. Later, if there are bursaries for a larger number, I would ask the heads of educational institutions, parish priests, nuns running orphanages, for recommendations. At the moment I know a number of schools which could be relied on to follow the wishes of the donors.

Q. *What kind of work would these children be eligible for?*
A. Boys who have been to school would get semi-skilled jobs in factories; for girls such jobs are now becoming available too. At the moment, social custom is against girls going out to work where they will have to mix with men, but this attitude is breaking down. There are opportunities for girls as nurses; until recently this would have been regarded as a Christian profession.

Q. *What would happen to the children if they do not go to school?*
A. If we do not educate them, they will remain sweepers, coolies, scavengers, i.e. they will not only get the dirty jobs but the treatment and housing that goes with them.

Q. *Will outcast children be accepted in schools?*

A. Harijan (pariah) children will be accepted in 'mixed' schools. Caste prejudice is still very strong but there is now no open discrimination against such children in school. Moreover, the richer people are generally the higher caste people, and these send their children to expensive schools out of touch with the poor.

Q. *Do the children need clothes and books?*

A. Clothes, books, religious objects would be of use, but the Customs present an almost insuperable obstacle so that, for the time being, such gifts are not practicable. Further, so many poor Indians are in debt that many such gifts fall immediately into the hands of money-lenders. Let us educate the children first.

Q. *What would be the cost of one such bursary?*

A. At elementary school level (Standards I-V) most of the children would go to day school. What is needed for these is enough for books, clothes, entrance fees and a few additional fees as well as possible fares. I recently found three children, aged 7-10, who walked ten miles per day to and from school. The Government helps Harijans at this stage, so that a bursary of £12 would just about do per year to keep them at school. The more of this type the better, since we would be helping the very poorest.

Because the poor live in such small rooms and so very overcrowded there can be no question of any study at home. Any higher studies would require boarding school. Costs vary according to the size of the township, but £50 per year would cover the cost of the cheaper ones. College education (university) would be £100. If possible it would be good if some of the Harijans went to university; it would help them to raise the standard of their poor community.

Q. *Could our bursaries, if any, be called after communities which gave them, thus helping to spread goodwill?*

A. There would be no difficulty in this. It is a very good idea. The children would certainly be told. The heads of institutions would administer each bursary.

Q. *Can we make certain that the money will be earmarked for your scheme only?*

A. Yes, the money would be for education only. We are not offering palliatives but trying to raise the next generation of outcasts so that they can find justice in life. You must remember that standards are much lower here. A B.A. here is only of the level of a school leaving certificate in England.

On November 2nd, 1962, the *Catholic Herald* very generously published the whole of this appeal. It ended with these three paragraphs:

Dear Reader,—You have the facts provided by an English priest who has worked in Southern India for thirty years. This priest goes further than the ordinary mission appeal. He sets out the case for contributions so that the outcast children may be educated, the only way in which we may lift the load of contempt and injustice which lies so heavily on these poor people, our brethren in the faith.

God has favoured our cause. At the very time when Fr Nevett was penning his appeal, I came up with a husband and wife, both British and both born in India. The Brigadier later served in India, coming back to Europe just in time to win a D.S.O. at Dunkirk. Both were received into the Church five years ago, both know India well, both agree that Fr Nevett's verdict on the plight of the Outcasts is if anything too mild.

They and their friends are willing to give the time to organize the scheme. They judge it practical and timely, offering to one small community in Southern India some future hope. It is to be hoped that many organizations, institutions, individual families in Britain will be willing to help to send bursaries.

The scheme will start in a small way, every donation, however small, will be personally acknowledged, every Indian child will be informed. Where possible information about the children will be sent to benefactors so that the Nevett scheme may not end in almsgiving but may grow into a genuine union between Christians in Britain and Madras. The address to be noted is: The Nevett Fund, 1, Albert Road, Bournemouth, Hants.

It was a joy to me in Rome during the session of the Council to receive a weekly record of the result of this appeal. It was a pleasure to speak to many Indian bishops and priests about it and to have their expert approval and commendation for all that we hoped to do. Ours was a small and limited scheme, confined to the generosity of readers of one weekly paper and to the Indian outcasts living in hutments below the level of that stinking and stagnant pond.

No final figures are available for publication in this book. After two months and two weeks, £1,300 had come, mostly in postal orders, and some twelve generous readers had promised a £12 bursary for five years.

One reader sent the whole prize won on a premium bond. Another not only sent money but gave us a codicil in his will. Two Scottish schools collected £12. One reader adopted an Indian boy in memory of her own child killed in an accident. The organizers give their time and all the postage so that the children may receive every penny that is sent.

As a religious, I myself have been unable to contribute any cash. Through the great generosity of my superiors, however, I have received permission to devote to the Nevett fund all the royalties earned through this book. This is a very considerable gesture of good will and approval from those who not only clothe and support me but who are themselves committed to vast charitable and missionary expenses in various parts of the world. I am grateful indeed for this permission, which provides some justification for this book. One would not like to use the General Council as a means of private profit and I would not have published these trivial essays in the normal course. But I am pleased as a priest to play the fool in my piazza that the outcast children of Madurai may go to school.

Thank you. may god bless you. Louis
thank you. May God bless you Frederick.

நான் உ ஙகளிஙகி ஐ அறி
ளோடு ததிகிறேன்.
மேரி

I'M grateful to you.Mary.(Tamil)